CITIZEN ZERO

The Assassination of Luis Donaldo Colosio

JESÚS ZAMORA PIERCE

Copyright © 2014, Jesús Zamora Pierce

All rights reserved.

ISBN: 1496145372
ISBN-13: 978-1496145376

DEDICATION

For my grandchildren Iker, Alvaro, Iñigo, Jerónimo and Maya.

CONTENTS

Note to the reader	1
The Crime	3
Death	17
The Two Aburtos	25
The Book of Records	36
Aburto	46
The Conspiracy	58
The Mastermind	70
Appendix	88

NOTE TO THE READER

It is not necessary to read this book. All the information it contains about the investigation on Colosio's assassination is in the official dockets. However, if the reader is not willing or does not have time to read 68,293 pages, this work may provide the reader with a summary of the investigation, the investigators themselves and their conclusions.

On the afternoon of May 14th, 1610, Henry IV, king of France, was heading in his coach from the Louvre to Arsenal, to visit Sully. Stalls along the way forced the king's vehicle to stop at *rue de la Ferronnerie*. He had forgotten his eyeglasses and was concentrated on listening to the Duke of Epernon, who was reading him a letter. The assassin, read-haired François Ravaillac, stands up on the axle of the right rear wheel, raises up to the level of the king and stabs him twice with a long knife, murdering him.

France was torn for years, between two opposing theories: Ravaillac was a solitary assassin, as he stated, or the crime was the result of a conspiracy.

Ravaillac was 32 years old

THE CRIME

The deep voice on the phone was that of a middle-aged man. His vocabulary and way of speaking were those of an educated person accustomed to giving orders. "You have been highly recommended," he said. "I want to ask you to be my advisor. I'm working in temporary offices for the time being." He gave me an address on Avenida Juárez. We agreed on an appointment on that same day. He didn't mention why he was requesting my assistance. It wasn't necessary as he had given me his name: Miguel Montes. All Mexico knew that President Carlos Salinas de Gortari had just designated him as Special Deputy Attorney General to investigate the murder of Luis Donaldo Colosio Murrieta. Montes offered me a front-row seat to observe the history of Mexico developing.

* * *

On Sunday morning, November 28th, 1993, the members of the National Executive Committee of the PRI met in the office adjacent to the library, in the presidential residence of Los Pinos. President Salinas had summoned them to organize the launch of the candidate for president of the Republic.

Public opinion had already identified, among the members of the cabinet, those who were most likely to be nominated: the secretary of Social Development, Donaldo Colosio; the Finance Minister, Pedro

Aspe; Manuel Camacho, Mayor of Mexico City; the Minister of Public Education, Ernesto Zedillo and Emilio Lozoya, Minister of Energy, Mines and State-owned Industry.

President Salinas spoke separately with some of the leaders of the PRI and then gathered them in his office.

As President Salinas himself narrates: "The consensus in favor of Colosio was evident. The national leaders of the PRI agreed to move immediately to the Party headquarters to disclose the nomination… Afterwards, I invited Donaldo to speak with me… To start the conversation, I told him that his performance was truly exceptional. He had managed to promote continuous change from within the system. I told him I knew of his commitment to the people, to work with the people and for the people. I also stressed that he understood the changes that the world was experiencing and was willing to undertake them. But I went no further. It was unnecessary to elaborate on the reasons for his candidacy. For several years, they had become apparent. I stopped. I looked him in the eyes. They were shining. He imagined what I was about to say, but it was not the same as knowing it. I was then overcome by emotion in a way that I had only experienced six years earlier, on October 2nd, 1987, when Miguel de la Madrid informed me that the PRI was going to nominate me as their candidate. Slowly but firmly, since I was convinced about his qualities and merits, I said: "Donaldo, the PRI will nominate you for President of the Republic". I was almost choked with emotion. Visibly moved, Donaldo asked me to stand up; he shook my hand and gave me a warm and long hug. He said he would undertake the challenge with conviction and courage. We talked for over two hours about the challenges that the country was facing, the allies and adversaries in the struggle, about the effort made and how much remained to be done. We talked about family life, the children and their future. His enthusiasm was evident. He vibrated with the energy of a long desired goal."

* * *

Being the PRI candidate to the presidency of the Republic ensured the triumph. However, the candidates complied with the ritual of traveling widely throughout the country, in order to be known and to learn firsthand about the problems of the country.

On March 7th, 1994 Guillermo Hopkins Gámez, Logistics Assistant Coordinator of the campaign, had completed the program for the activities of the final week of the first stage of Colosio's campaign. The candidate would visit the Northwest of the country, comprising the states of Sinaloa on March 22nd, Baja California Sur at noon on March 23rd, Baja California on the evening of the 23rd and all day on March 24th, and Sonora on March 25th and 26th.

The schedule for the visit to the city of Tijuana, was as follows:

1. 15:00 hours – Arrival at Tijuana airport.
2. 15:10 hours – Departure from the airport.
3. 15:25 hours – Arrival at Lomas Taurinas (Dialogue with residents).
4. 16:25 hours – Departure from Lomas Taurinas.
5. 18:30 hours – Arrival at "Club Campestre" (Dialogue with teachers).
6. 19:30 hours – Departure from meeting.
7. 21:00 hours – Arrival at "Salón Modular" of the "Grand Hotel" (Dinner with representatives of the civil society).
8. 22:30 hours – Departure from dinner.
9. 22:35 hours – Arrival at hotel for overnight stay.

In his draft agenda, Colosio made some handwritten notes. He circled the words "Lomas Taurinas".

* * *

On March 17, 1994, Guillermo Hopkins Gámez traveled to Tijuana to meet with the Municipal Committee of the PRI to agree on the place where Colosio would meet with the residents of that city. After considering other proposals such as El Terrenazo, El Florido, the racecourse, the bullring, the esplanade of the PRI, the ejido Mariano Matamoros and a sports club, as proposed by Jaime Martínez Veloz, they decided to have the gathering at Lomas Taurinas, a neighborhood where the solidarity program had been very successful, it was especially supportive of the PRI and represented the characteristics of Tijuana: low socioeconomic conditions, and was located near the airport.

That same day, Hopkins Gámez visited Lomas Taurinas.

There was only one paved street to reach the square where they intended to hold the event. It was necessary to park the car at the end of this street and continue on foot. The street was interrupted by a stream of sewage that could only be crossed by walking on a wooden board 7 meters long by 2.80 meters wide. Juan Maldonado Pereda warned that crossing the wooden bridge was dangerous, since it had no guardrails and the floor was rough plywood. It risked braking with the weight of the crowd, and due to its narrowness someone could fall off. Others commented that the bridge was fragile and dangerous and that it seemed it was neither safe nor strong enough to withstand the crossing of many people at the same time. However, Jorge Schiaffino Isunza stated that the bridge strength had been checked and, after confirming that it was strong enough, they decided not to modify its surface, since the campaign mangers did not want to present the candidate in scenes that were not real.

After crossing the bridge, it was necessary to travel about fifty meters over unpaved, uneven and rocky-sloped terrain in disrepair, in order to get to the place that the local PRI had chosen for Colosio to address the residents.

Hopkins Gámez suggested that the pavilion from where Colosio would talk should be located on the lowest part of the land, in order to facilitate his exit after the meeting.

Several members of the PRI Municipal Committee disagreed considering that Lomas Taurinas was not a suitable place.

* * *

On March 23rd, 1994, between six and seven o'clock in the morning, the activity caused by the partisan act began at Lomas Taurinas. José Israel Andrade Mora and José Luis Chávez Sánchez, supervisor and operator of the sound equipment began to install it with the help of four more people. They placed the speakers on stones, one on top of the other, due to the fact that they were not carrying scaffolding and were not able to get any, four speakers on the right side and four on the left, four monitors, two on each side, and racks that were installed behind each speaker. Once the equipment was installed, the Presidential Security Staff arrived and ordered some changes for security reasons, both regarding the equipment and the candidate, giving instructions to leave an emergency exit in case any unexpected problems could arise, so the equipment should not be in the way. It took about four hours to install the equipment.

Yldefonso Cardoso Gálvez, coordinator of the National Solidarity Program in the Mesa de Otay, in Tijuana arrived in the morning. He decided it would be convenient for Colosio to address the public from the top of a pick-up platform, which would give him greater visibility. He sent several assistants to ask who was the owner of a very old, grey pick-up truck that was parked on Punta street. They found out that it belonged to Juan Manuel Barrón, who gave his consent for Colosio to climb on it for the meeting. Cardoso ordered the car to be moved a few meters in order to place it on the originally selected site, i.e., on the upper part of the esplanade.

Also during the morning, different security groups arrived: fifteen elements from the Presidential Security Staff, seventeen elements under the command of Fernando de la Sota Rodalleguez, who had been hired by General Domiro García Reyes, responsible for Colosio's security, and twenty volunteers gathered by José Rodolfo Rivapalacio Tinajero, appointed by the PRI in Tijuana, to assist in the formation of barriers to control the crowd, to watch people crossing the wooden bridge in order to prevent them from falling from it, to make sure that there were no trouble-making groups, to keep vehicles clear from the access ramp to the neighborhood and to expedite the movement of vehicles.

* * *

General Domiro García Reyes hired Fernando de la Sota

Rodalleguez to join the security team of the campaign. De la Sota, in turn, had assembled a team of about 160 people. He sent 34 to Mazatlán and 98 to Culiacán. He took 28 people to Tijuana, 17 for Lomas Taurinas and 11 for Club Campestre. He arrived in Tijuana on March 22nd, 1994, at 16:30 hours. They stayed at the Jabalolla Hotel. All the staff gathered at 19:00 hours. He gave them the order to have dinner and to get ready for the next day.

On March 23rd, at 11:30 hours, De la Sota and 28 of his men went to Lomas Taurinas, where they arrived at 12:00 o'clock. Once there, the 28 members of the group tested the strength of the bridge, they proceeded to clear the area of street vendors and cars that were parked on the access street, telling the residents to remove their vehicles in order to allow easy access for Colosio. De la Sota sent 11 members to Club Campestre, keeping 17 at Lomas Taurinas, whom he distributed by placing three at the entrance or street crossings, to start forming the barrier, three other elements were placed at the site, fifty or sixty meters ahead a cordon was placed to stop the people once the candidate had passed through, in order to keep the crowd away from him, four members were placed here; further, before crossing the bridge, he located four members to prevent people from crossing the bridge on mass; he also located three members in the lower part, to the left of the pavilion.

Héctor Javier Hernández Tomassiny was among the men who arrived with De la Sota to Lomas Taurina. This young man had dreamed of studying at the Polytechnic, but he had to put aside those plans when he got married on January 29th, 1994. Marriage forced him to earn an income and he started working as a messenger for an accounting firm, with a monthly salary of $700.00 new pesos. When his wife informed him that she was pregnant, he felt the urgent need to make more money. His uncle, Roberto Tomassiny Ortiz introduced him to his friend De la Sota, who hired him. On March 20th he was instructed to go to the Observatorio bus station, where he departed at 22:00 hours bound for Tijuana to fulfill his first commitment in his new job.

* * *

Yolanda Lázaro Caratachea lived in Lomas Taurinas, at 13626 Carlos Salinas de Gortari street. She was the leader of the neighborhood, a militant and member of the municipal council of the PRI. On March 23rd, she left her home at approximately 10:00 hours, accompanied by Juvenal Bañuelos, head of the block, and they toured the neighborhood in a truck, inviting the people to attend the event. About eleven o'clock in the morning, a person claiming to be the coordinator of Colosio's campaign, stopped her and told her that, according to Colosio's instructions, he did not want the PRI to be mentioned. Lázaro Caratachea replied "We are tired of people coming from outside to coordinate us. This is my home and I'm going to invite my colleagues," and continued her work. About half an hour later the same person stopped her insisting that this was not a political act. Lázaro Caratachea got out of the truck and confronted him, "I'm fed up! I don't understand why I cannot say PRI, since he is the candidate of the PRI. And, why is this not a political act?" There was no one to stop Yolanda, she and other PRI supporters started pasting propaganda with Colosio's picture and the words "Vote for the PRI". But, as soon as they finished, four unknown men withdrew the propaganda stating that the candidate did not want anything ostentatious or that looked like PRI, they even took away their caps with Colosio's name on them.

At around 15:00 hours, approximately, she saw some young people arriving with a sign that said "Colosio, Camacho and Marcos are watching you", on one side, and on the back it said "No more PRI government. Say no to Televisa". The residents started arguing with those carrying the sign; they did not come to blows, but took the sign from them and tore it. At that time security personnel arrived and ended the confrontation.

* * *

Sara Ruth Martínez Meraz was the social promoter of the PRI's territorial movement; she lived in Subdelegación Florido Mariano, Delegación de la Presa, in the Municipality of Tijuana. She learned of Colosio's arrival a couple of days before. At the party's offices, she got flyers that she handed out inviting people to attend the meeting. On March 23rd, those in her neighborhood – around 200 people –

went to Avenida de las Torres and got in in different vehicles to go to Tijuana, arriving at Lomas Taurinas at around 15:00 hours. Martínez Meraz took her two young daughters with her.

* * *

Tranquilino Sánchez Venegas was a 57-year-old man, born in Guadalajara, Jalisco, now living in Tijuana, where he had a poor economic status due to his education. He had only reached the fourth grade.

On March 23rd, he went to Calle Cuarta to pay his water bill and headed down Avenida Revolución to the PRI headquarters, which are located at the end of this avenue, adjacent to the international border separating Mexico from the USA. At the door of the PRI's offices, he met Rodolfo Rivapalacio Tinajero, whom he had known for 35 years. Rivapalacio told him it was good he had arrived and asked him to help him with Colosio's security, who was visiting Tijuana in a few hours. Sánchez Venegas accepted. Rivapalacio gave him a badge and a piece of paper with instructions on how all those in charge of candidate's security should behave. He told him to treat well those attending the act, not to push them and that there should be no violence at any time. Rivapalacio ordered two young men that had a vehicle to transport Sánchez Venegas and other security staff members that were at the party's offices, to Lomas Taurinas.

* * *

Sixty-year old Vicente Mayoral Valenzuela had been an agent of the State Judicial Police for many years, but he had quit a couple of years before. He was then employed by a real estate company and now worked in the food business.

On March 21st, he went with his son Rodolfo Mayoral Esquer to the PRI offices to greet a friend. They found Rodolfo Rivapalacio Tinajero at the door and greeted him. After a short exchange of pleasantries, Rivapalacio sought their help. On March 23rd, the candidate of the PRI to the Presidency of the Republic would visit Tijuana. Rivapalacio was responsible for organizing a group of people who would be in charge of Colosio's security and he had only gathered three people. The Mayorals agreed to be the fourth and the fifth elements.

On March 23rd, at 12:00 hours, the Mayorals showed up again outside the PRI offices, where they found Rivapalacio, along with others who would also participate in security tasks. Rivapalacio gave them hurried instructions and the Mayorals went to Lomas Taurinas in their Volkswagen. They arrived after 12:30 hours. They proudly carried a white cloth badge that said SECURITY, given to them by Rivapalacio a few minutes before,

Following Rivapalacio's instructions, Mayoral spotted Roberto Cárdenas, who told him that the Security Operation consisted of keeping order among the attendees, so that they would not invade the corridor through which Colosio would arrive.

* * *

Numerous cameramen also arrived at Lomas Taurinas with the mission of filming the meeting for various television news programs, information agencies and the PRI. Cameramen sent by the Federal Judicial Police in Tijuana were stationed on top of a dwelling, getting an excellent view of the area where the meeting would take place.

* * *

Colosio arrived in Tijuana shortly after 16:00 hours, in a private plane, from La Paz, Baja California Sur. He was accompanied by General Domiro García Reyes and Major Germán González Castillo. Senator César Moreno welcomed him and explained that about 1500 people were waiting for him at the airport. This was an unexpected number, since no call had been made. It was very difficult for Colosio to leave the airport as people crowded around him to deliver letters and shake his hand. It took him about fifteen minutes to cover the few yards to the Blazer truck that he used for transportation. He asked senator Moreno if there was a microphone available so he could address the people that had met there. The senator answered that due to the tight schedule, no act had been scheduled at the airport. The candidate then stepped on the side step of the Blazer and waived to all the attendees.

Colosio then got in the Blazer truck, seating next to the driver. General García Reyes was behind the driver, Mr. Juan Maldonado Pereda in the middle, and senator César Moreno behind Colosio.

The convoy was led by a Spirit car, driven by Lieutenant Humberto Ojinaga Ruiz, accompanied by Major Germán González Castillo; then followed the candidate's Blazer truck, thirdly a Suburban truck where Major Víctor Manuel Cantú Monterrubio and Lieutenants Martín Salinas Reyes, Roberto Merín Sandoval and Miguel Ángel Zimbrón López, were traveling; all of them belonging to the candidate's security group. At the rear of the convoy there was a fourth vehicle, called the "emergency car," in the event that the candidate's vehicle had a break down, and lastly a Suburban with the work team.

The distance between the airport and Lomas Taurinas was traveled in approximately fifteen minutes. When reaching the ramp down to the neighborhood, a spontaneous vehicle usher told them that there was no room beyond. The driver of the Blazer stopped completely and Colosio got out and started walking alone, surprising his companions, who had quickly exited the vehicle and ran to catch up with him. It was 16:30 hours.

The members of his escort were grouped around Colosio, in a diamond formation, with Major Cantú ahead, Lieutenant Zimbrón behind the candidate, Lieutenant Salinas on his left and Lieutenant Merin on his right, while Colonel Pancardo and General García kept a variable position with regard to Colosio because of the uneven terrain. In this way they got to the wooden bridge, they crossed it and headed down Mariano Arista street up to the pavilion, namely the pick-up truck that served as a pavilion, where the candidate stepped on.

Before Colosio's speech, five speakers took the floor: Sofía Colín Mercado, leader of Lomas Taurinas and coordinator of the Solidarity Committee, José Luis Gasca, from the Territorial Movement in

Ensenada; Jorge Luis Gutiérrez Domínguez, from the *Unión de Colonos de Infonavit Hidalgo*, in Tecate; Edmundo Frutos, who was doing his social service in the Ministry of Social Development in Otay and Yolanda Lázaro Caratachea, Lomas Taurinas leader as well, and member of the Municipal Council. Afterwards, the candidate gave his speech and the act concluded, in approximately 35 minutes, around 17:08 hours.

* * *

When the ceremony was over, Vicente Mayoral Valenzuela and his son Rodolfo Mayoral Esquer, as well as other volunteers from the local PRI tried to form a barrier to facilitate the candidate's exit, but Colosio stepped down from the pick-up on the opposite side of the barrier. So he landed in the middle of a crowd of three thousand five hundred people. The narrow wooden bridge prevented their exit. Most of them didn't want to go out anyway, they wanted to approach the candidate for an autograph, to say hello, hand him a request, or just touch he who would be President of Mexico. The uneven terrain hindered further the progress of the candidate. The sound system was blasting at full volume the song "La Culebra", emphasizing the sense of disorder.

Yolanda Lázaro Caratachea was struggling forward, walking about a meter behind Colosio, when she saw a man in a black jacket pulling something out of his jacket. Lázaro Caratachea thought it was a document. Tranquilino Sánchez Venegas was walking in front of her and raised his hand. Above Tranquilino's semi-flexed arm, Yolanda sees Mario Aburto (the man in the black jacket) putting the gun close to Colosio's right ear and shooting. Colosio, wounded, moves his arms, apparently trying to reach his head and begins to fall, spinning on his own axis. At that time, Mario Aburto shoots for the second time. Yolanda lost all sense of time, place and orientation. She walked a few more meters like a sleepwalker. Recovering, she finds herself facing Vicente Mayoral Valenzuela, who had a gun in his hand, and looked also disoriented. "You killed him, you killed him" Yolanda yelled. Her screams seemed to wake up Vicente, who replied, "I did not kill him. I took the gun away from him."

* * *

Sara Ruth Martínez Meraz was walking behind the candidate, to his right. A man who was trying to organize the people puts an arm over her right shoulder, making her go back. At this time she hears a shot, looks up and sees Mario Aburto with a gun in his right hand. She sees Aburto moving forward and shooting a falling Colosio for the second time.

Sara's two younger daughters were walking on Colosio's left, behind him. So, when Aburto shoots a second time, Sara shouts, desperately, thinking he had wounded one of her daughters, since as Colosio falls down, Sara can also see one of her daughters on the floor. At that time, Sara was seized by a hysterical attack and ran back and forth screaming in anguish.

* * *

Once Colosio descended from the pavilion, Mónica Lizeth Torres Martínez moved to his left side, but the crowd forced her to move to his right flank, just beside him. She saw Aburto moving among the people until he was beside Colosio, and raised his hand with the gun. Mónica tried to shout so someone would push the candidate, but she could not utter a sound. She saw Aburto shoot Colosio in the head. Only then could she scream. She heard a second shot and fainted falling to the ground.

* * *

Fernando de la Sota Rodalleguez is walking about a meter and a half behind Colosio when he hears two shots and sees Aburto holding the gun and pointing towards the ground.

Fernando springs at Aburto. He skips over Colosio's fallen body and holds Aburto by the arm, while he grabs Vicente Mayoral Valenzuela with his left hand. In the struggle, the three fell down.

At that moment, Major Cantú came closer, wielding a gun and asking De la Sota who had fired the shot. De la Sota, who was in shock, could not speak, he merely pointed at Aburto. The latter, pointing at Mayoral, said: "It was the old guy, it was the old guy."

* * *

Alejandro García Hinojosa, who belonged to the De la Sota group, was walking behind Colosio, trying to keep people from throwing themselves on the candidate, without any success. He heard the detonation of a gun and turned towards the direction of the sound. The people, moved by fear, had opened a circle around Aburto. In that fleeting stage, García Hinojosa sees Aburto with the gun in his hand. He sees De la Sota throwing himself on Aburto and he follows him, rushing against Aburto. Then a second shot is heard. Everything happens in a split of a second.

De la Sota and García Hinojosa fall almost simultaneously on Aburto, knocking him down.

* * *

Vicente Mayoral Valenzuela was pushing people that wanted to greet the candidate, in order to make way from him. He was behind the candidate, about a meter and a half or two meters away. When he heard the gunshot, he immediately turned towards the blast, seeing Aburto with the gun in his hand. He rushed against Aburto, holding him by the wrist of the hand with the gun and forcing him to point the gun towards the floor. At that time someone held Aburto from behind and then more people were upon them, all of them falling down. This caused Aburto to drop the weapon that ended up a few centimeters away. Some people thought Mayoral was the aggressor, so they pulled his hair and threw punches at him, in confusion.

* * *

When Colosio stepped down from the pick-up, General Domiro García Reyes was behind him and began struggling to follow him in the middle of the crowd. A burly man, wearing a jacket, carrying a white emblem, stands in his way, preventing him from moving forward. At that time he hears a gunshot. He catches sight of a gun. He manages to elude the guy in the jacket and finds Colosio, lying face down on the ground, in a pool of blood. It was 17:12 hours.

On April 14th, 1865, President Lincoln, accompanied by his wife and two guests was in a box at the Ford Theater in Washington, D.C., attending a theatrical performance.

John Wilkes Booth came into the box, shooting a Philadelphia Deringer, wounding Lincoln in the head and killing him.

Booth was part of a conspiracy that supported the Confederate Cause. The murderer was chased and killed by the army. He was 27 years old.

DEATH

General Domiro García Reyes rushed over to Colosio and turned him on his back. At that time, Colosio shook, and a stream of blood and brain matter came out from the bullet hole. Lieutenants Miguel Ángel Zimbrón López, Martín Salinas Reyes and Roberto Merín Sandoval, the candidate's escorts, picked him up and carried him across the wooden bridge. The vehicle closest to the bridge was the Blazer truck. They got him in it, got in themselves, as well as Lieutenant Humberto Francisco Ojinaga Ruíz, major Germán González Castillo and doctor Guillermo Alberto Castorena Arellano, the candidate's personal physician.

The driver of the Blazer, Nolberto Hernández Acosta, started the vehicle.

An ambulance was parked in an alley, opposite to the wooden bridge, the driver was Juan Sabino Venegas. It was there due to an agreement between the municipal PRI and the General Hospital in order to provide support in case of an emergency. The ambulance was equipped with intensive care equipment, i.e., ventilator, ambu, laryngoscope, sera, contained in what is medically known as a "red wagon". Sabino had been instructed by Helio Lara, head of ambulances of the General Hospital, to wait in a street near the pavilion, but he considered it was not the right place, due to the nature of the place, so he decided to park the ambulance in the alley.

Seeing a group of people carrying someone and putting him in the Blazer, he started the ambulance and, with the open siren, tried to reach the truck that was heading for the exit. It was difficult for him to drive the ambulance, since the trucks of the motorcade were on Mimiahuapan street partially blocking the way, so he drove on the curb and was able to pass the caravan on the right and reached the Blazer approximately 500 meters ahead.

The Blazer stopped and its occupants put Colosio in the ambulance. At that time, the ambulance driver, Juan Sabino Venegas, realized that the injured person was Colosio. Before closing the rear doors of the ambulance, he asked where he was going. Doctor Álvaro García Taxilaga said "To the General Hospital".

During the brief, very brief minutes that the trip lasted, Doctor García Taxilaga, who belonged to the Presidential Staff and had been commissioned to the candidate's campaign, carried out resuscitation maneuvers, introduced a Guedel airway for ventilation and started an IV for supplying saline. While giving him first aid, he realized that Colosio had severe bilateral mydriasis, a sign of severe brain damage. His medical experience told him that his patient was brain dead and had only cardiac and respiratory functions.

Doctor Guillermo Alberto Castorena Arellano, Colosio's personal physician and Doctor Luis Alonso Villegas Cuervo, doctor in charge of ambulance Delta 7 of the General Hospital of Tijuana were also in the ambulance. The three doctors, without exchanging a single word, were busy helping the patient. While carrying out mouth-to-mouth resuscitation maneuvers, Doctor Castorena realized that the patient had also an injury in the abdomen. Doctor Villegas took the blood pressure.

The admission note of the clinical record states that Colosio entered the Emergency Room of the Tijuana General Hospital at 17:20 hours and he was medically described as follows:

"…found unconscious with symptoms that had started 10 minutes before, showing a medical condition with loss of consciousness, apparent gunshot wounds in the skull and abdomen... Vital signs were: blood pressure 90/50, heart rate 110 per minute and absent respiratory rate, physical examination showed generalized pallor of teguments, without respiratory automatism, active bleeding from oral cavity and bilateral otorrhagia. Head: gunshot wound in the right temple and left parietal region, anisocoria, tachycardia; abdomen wound located in the left upper quadrant; extremities with slow capillary refill, integrating the diagnoses of gunshot injuries in skull and abdomen, and shock".

Doctor Castorena reports that Colosio underwent two simultaneous surgeries: exploratory laparotomy of the abdomen by doctors Álvaro García Taxilaga and Sergio Mascareño and a craniotomy performed by neurosurgeons Felipe Tovar Vázquez, Jesús Machado Salas and Enrique Sánchez Varela.

Three general practitioners participated in Colosio's medical care, five internists, three neurosurgeons, two cardiologists and five anesthesiologists.

The cardiologist Patricia Aubanel Riedel was invited to the operating room where the group of doctors, nurses and assistants were attending Colosio, she got the patient's condition overview through an analysis and a quick cardiovascular assessment, who was highly unstable at the edge of cardiac arrest. She applied intravenous drugs to stimulate the heart rate and increase blood pressure, and simultaneous blood transfusions. She opened percutaneous venous pathways on the femoral and bilateral veins in order to bring these drugs faster to the patient in the necessary volumes. Not having favorable responses in increasing his vital signs, she proceeded, by one of the left femoral venous lines to pass a pacemaker catheter into the right ventricle of the heart in order to artificially increase the heart contractions, trying to raise the blood pressure, while maneuvering to achieve this, she applied a transcutaneous pacemaker in the patient's chest area. Vital signs (blood pressure and heart rate), did not respond to these maneuvers. The patient's pulse disappeared completely even though the monitor showed an impaired rate of forty per minute, this is called electromechanical dissociation, which means an almost irreversible fact and a terminal forecast.

* * *

When he threw himself on Aburto, De la Sota fell on his head towards the bottom of the slope. He was helped up and, along with Mayor Cantú, Lt. Col. Pancardo and Alejandro García Hinojosa, who was holding Aburto by the neck, led him under arrest. The crowd followed them, insulting Aburto, hitting him, throwing stones at him and shouting "Kill him, kill him!"

Crossing the bridge, De la Sota lost sight of those who carried Aburto. He turned back to look for Mayoral, the "old man" who Aburto identified as the gunman. He spotted him, he was walking with his jacket slung on his shoulder, he asked him to accompany him and, he transferred him, in a press van, to the Attorney General's Office.

Those who had arrested Aburto made their way with difficulty through the crowd, leading him to a Suburban truck that Colonel Reynaldos del Pozo had got. He took the driver's position; Lt. Col. Pancardo sat to his left, in the middle seat to the left, the vehicle owner and on the right, Víctor Manuel Cantú Monterrubio, and in the back seat Alejandro García Hinojosa and Aburto.

The people, swirling around the truck, prevented the vehicle from moving forward and threw stones at it, breaking one of the windows. They finally managed to start moving and got to a paved road, but were intercepted by elements of the Tactical Group, one of whom, pointing an AK-47 at Colonel Reynaldos ordered him to identify himself. He did, and then, the police helped clear the way and escorted them, with one vehicle in front and another one behind, to the Attorney General's Office, where they arrived at approximately 17:50 hours.

Aburto was taken to the Federal Judicial Police area, where he stayed, seating in a chair, in Commander Alfredo Cuadros Aldana's office, guarded by Carlos Arturo Pancardo Escudero, Víctor Manuel Cantú Rubio and Federico Antonio Reynaldos del Pozo, who were joined by Raúl Loza Parra, and agents Arturo Piña Pérez and César Gamboa by orders of the Deputy Delegate of the Federal Judicial

Police.

In the meantime, Commander Hernández Vergara, aware of the crowd's behavior at Lomas Taurinas, ordered security measures to protect the building against any possible attack on Aburto.

Immediately, two experts from the Attorney General's Office and an expert from the Attorney General of the State focused on establishing if there were lead and barium residues in Mayoral's and Aburto's hands, as a result of shooting a fire arm. They underwent the Harrison Gilroy test (sodium radizonate), which showed the presence of lead and barium in Aburto's hands, but not in Mayoral's hands. Aburto had fired a gun.

* * *

In the afternoon of March 23rd, President Salinas was in the Vicente Guerrero room of the main office at Los Pinos, in a meeting with farmers. The meeting ended at approximately 19:30 hours (given the time difference it was 17:30 hours in Tijuana). When they left the room, General Arturo Cardona and the head of the President's Office, José Córdoba, immediately approached the President with the news: Colosio had suffered an attack. He had been shot and was in a hospital where doctors were struggling to save his life. He was deeply disturbed. He tried to recover. He went upstairs to his office. He called Doctor Enrique Wolpert, deputy Secretary of Health, who had a close relationship with Colosio. He asked him to travel immediately to Tijuana and to take the best specialist with him.

He also spoke over the network with the Attorney General, Diego Valadés, and instructed him to go to Tijuana immediately.

* * *

In Tijuana, the Federal Public Prosecutor Jesús Romero Magaña started drafting a document for Aburto's declaration. He stated that it was 19:30 hours on March 23rd, 1994. He informed Aburto that the reason for his detention were the injuries that apparently he had inflicted on Colosio by shooting a gun at him.

Aburto said he was willing to testify. Mr. Romero Magaña informed him that he had the right to appoint a lawyer or someone he trusted to assist him. He said he had neither someone he trusted nor a lawyer and the Prosecutor appointed Mr. Xavier Alfonso Carbajal Machado, Chairman of the "Emilio Rabasa" Bar of Tijuana, as his lawyer.

Aburto then declared:

"That the one speaking, as previously mentioned, was living in the city of Zamora, Michoacán, until about the age of fifteen, remembering this because it was then when he finished his secondary education, leaving his house, because he had various pacifist ideas, he lived in several states of Mexico where he met with a group of people of different political views and different social status, the person declaring also being known by the nickname of "CABALLERO AGUILA" (EAGLE KNIGHT), which means an award; likewise states that he studied in a seminar, since he wanted to become a priest, but he quit because he was going to be sent to Puerto Rico, and he arrived in this city in the year eighty-six or eighty-seven, where he worked in a factory as production supervisor and currently he had been working for a month as a mechanic in the company called Camero Magnéticos, located at 426 Sebastián Vizcaíno, Fraccionamiento Garitas de Otay, and that in relation to the facts he states: That the person speaking had been preparing to injure the candidate to the Presidency of the Republic, MR. LUIS DONALDO COLOSIO MURRIETA, in a shooting camp in this city, where he fires different fire arms, he also remembers that in order to achieve his goal he purchased a thirty-eight caliber pistol, from a person whose name he will not give, stating in this act that it was his intention to hurt the aforementioned candidate, in order to get the attention of the press and expose his pacifist ideas, as well as the information he has about various armed groups that are located in different states of Mexico, since he has personally met with these groups where he came to know their ideas, and he also recalls that when he shot the candidate he was pushed by one someone who was there, and was able to fire two shots with the gun he was holding, and at that time some people in civilian clothes arrested him, together with policemen from the Federal Judicial Police, who were there, and was taken to the Federal Judicial Police offices in this city."

At that time, the .38 special revolver type gun, with chambers for six cartridges, with registration number 958400, as well as two good cartridges and two spent ones were shown to him, and Aburto declared: "That he recognizes such gun as the one he was carrying and which he had referred to in this statement and which is the one he used to shoot MR. LUIS DONALDO COLOSIO".

* * *

At the same time that Aburto was acknowledging having shot Colosio, the latter died in the General Hospital.

Resuscitation maneuvers had been carried out during an hour to an hour and a quarter to no avail. A quick dialogue among the responsible doctors led them to decide to stop these maneuvers. Colosio died at 19:45 hours.

On June 28th, 1914, at about eleven o'clock Archduke France Ferdinand of Austria and his wife were killed in Sarajevo, capital of the Austro-Hungarian province of Bosnia Herzegovina, by Gavrilo Princip, a Serbian extremist and one of several murderers hired by Black Hand, a Serbian terrorist group.

The Archduke was touring the city in an open *Gräf & Stift Double Phaeton*. Coincidently, Gavrilo Princip, who was in a café, recognizes him. The car passes by. But the driver, realizing he is lost, goes back and stops a few meters away from Princip. He draws his gun and shoots twice.

The crime, known as the Sarajevo Assassination, was one of the causes of First World War. Princip was 20 years old.

THE TWO ABURTOS

After Colosio's death, his wife, Diana Laura Riojas, authorized the autopsy. It started at 21:30 hours, at the amphitheater of the General Hospital.

The autopsy reports that the body shows two impacts by gunfire as follows:

1. An 11 mm diameter entry orifice on the right supra-auricular region, traveling from right to left, moderately from back to front and unobtrusively from the bottom up, with an exit orifice in the left tempora-parietal region which is involved in the surgical wound for craniotomy.

2. An entry orifice by gun fire in the abdominal region, at the epigastric level, 6.3 centimeters left of the middle line, measuring 9 mm in diameter, showing a left to right path, slightly from top to bottom, with exit at the right upper quadrant, 97 mm from the anterior midline. This wound did not penetrate the abdominal cavity.

The determining cause of death was the wound that perforated the skull, with positive Benassi sign, resulting from the explosion of gunpowder and proof that the murder weapon was in close proximity to his victim.

The autopsy was performed by Dr. Gustavo Salazar Fernández and Dr. Jesús Ramón Escajadillo Díaz from the Legal Medical Service of the Superior Court of Justice, by Dr. Esteban Chapital Gutiérrez from the Attorney General's Office of the State, by Dr. Alonso Villegas Cuervo from the Ministry of Health, and by Dr. Antonio Iván Muñoz Lara from the Attorney General of the Republic.

The autopsy concluded at approximately 0:30 am on March 24th. The body was embalmed and taken to Tijuana airport. There, presidential airplane number three, sent by President Salinas, was waiting. Colosio's widow, Diana Laura Riojas, traveled with him. The airplane took off at 3:00 am, it was 5:00 am in Mexico City.

At 8:00 am, President Salinas and his wife received Diana Laura at the presidential hangar. They traveled by car to the PRI headquarters. Salinas suggested to Diana Laura that Santiago Oñate Laborde should take charge of the murder investigation. The widow asked that the special prosecutor office be headed by the Supreme Court Justice Miguel Montes, a lawyer who had been very close to Colosio. Salinas immediately accepted. Shortly after, having obtained Montes' agreement, he issued a decree creating the Special Deputy Attorney General Office in charge of investigating Colosio's murder. Montes requested a temporary leave from the Supreme Court and assumed his new responsibility.

* * *

Aburto was transferred to Mexico City on a six-seater plane of the Attorney General's Office that arrived at the "Benito Juárez" International Airport on March 24th, at 14:30 hours. He was transferred to the Attorney General's Office and then to Almoloya de Juárez prison, in the State of Mexico, where his entry was registered at 00:35 hours on March 25th, 1994.

* * *

I met Montes in the temporary offices that had been provided for him on Avenida Juárez. The premises looked more like a furniture store. A large number of wooden desks made it difficult to get through, but it was impossible to work because there were no chairs.

I knew Montes had been Attorney General and was a Supreme Court Justice until he asked for leave to take charge as Special Prosecutor. I met then a fair-skinned, stocky man, with thinning hair and mustache, who seemed to be a little over fifty, speaking slowly about the serious responsibility he had accepted. He mentioned the names of some people who had agreed to join his team: Rafael Moreno González; Mario Crosswell Arenas, experienced investigator, Commander Emilio Islas Rangel, General Director of the National Central Bureau of Interpol, and other equally valuable elements. He asked me to advise him on all criminal and criminal procedural law.

I identified Montes as a man with principles and values and I accepted to be his advisor. I only asked, and he accepted, to be hired as an external advisor. I didn't want to become a public servant or leave my profession.

It was necessary to start working immediately because the press stated that the Aburto arrested at Lomas Taurinas and the one at Almoloya were different persons. There were two Aburtos.

* * *

The images of Aburto spread by the press and the television showed a man with messy, slightly curly hair, a thin mustache and a bloody face. When Aburto was presented to the press, in Almoloya, journalists saw a young man with short styled hair, and a clean, shaved face, without mustache.

The suspicion spread like wildfire; they had changed Aburto. There were two Aburtos: one who has arrested in Lomas Taurinas and another, a different one, who was now in prison in Almoloya. These multiple Aburtos provided grounds for elaborating all kinds of theories about the murder and were a story that would sell many newspapers.

* * *

Juan Pablo de Tavira, Director of Social Rehabilitation of the Ministry of Internal Affairs, reported that the hair differences between "the two Aburtos" were because Aburto had had a haircut and his mustache had been shaved when he was admitted to Almoloya, a procedure followed with all interns on admission day, in accordance to the Basic Comprehensive Procedures Manual of the High Security Penitentiary of Almoloya de Juárez. This bureaucratic explanation did not satisfy the press. The prosecution had to scientifically prove that Aburto was Aburto.

* * *

Rafael Moreno González studied medicine and graduated as a doctor. But fate took him in another direction, and little by little, he became a criminalist. As a teenager, he left his native province and traveled to Mexico City to continue his studies. He lived for 9 years with his uncle, Doctor Celestino Porte Petit, a great expert in criminal law and professor for many years. The young medical student had the opportunity to listen to the discussions held by the great criminal law experts of the time. The second influence that marked him was his professor, Doctor Alfonso Quiroz Cuarón, and the third one, a deep and decisive one, was a character that did not even exist: Sherlock Holmes. Moreno González, in conferences and books, has cited dozens of times a phrase by Sherlock Holmes which is key to criminal investigation: "Eliminate all other factors, and the one which remains must be the truth."

After graduating, Moreno González went to work for the expert services of the Attorney General's Office of the Federal District, where he gradually escalated positions. During the 1970s, Attorney General Sergio García Ramírez appoints him Director General of Expert Evidence and Moreno González decides that those services must have a scientific level and must adopt technological advances. The first step is a course for all expert services employees. Some of the speakers were Doctors Ruy Pérez Tamayo, Jesús Kumate, Felipe Pardinas Illanes and Carlos Biro Rosenbleuth. Afterwards, with support from the Department of Advanced Studies of UNAM, Moreno González gets his experts to be trained in the use of the necessary instruments for examining evidence: ultraviolet, infrared and gas chromatography and microphotography. Years later, under Attorney General, Ignacio Morales Lechuga's guidance, Moreno González brings the DNA (Deoxyribonucleic Acid) technique to Mexico, which allows coroners to identify the perpetrator, through a DNA analysis of blood, semen, skin, saliva or hair samples from the crime scene. With Moreno González the modern era of criminology in Mexico was born.

* * *

In 1880, English scientists Henry Faulds and William James Herschel sent a letter to the scientific journal *Nature*, claiming that the fingerprints of an individual are unique. Their observations were experimentally verified by English scientist Sir Francis Galton, who suggested the first elemental system for classifying fingerprints. The Galton system was developed by Sir Edward R. Henry. In 1901, Scotland Yard adopted this system as an indispensable instrument for identifying criminals.

In 1888 the Argentinean Juan Vucetich, an employee of the Buenos Aires Police Department, developed an original fingerprint classification system that he published in his book Compared Dactyloscopy in 1904. His system is the one currently used in most Spanish-speaking countries.

Fingerprints are the impression made by the ridges of the skin overlaying the fingers. It is a foolproof personal identification method because the design form on each finger of each human being is unique and unrepeatable, and is not altered by growth or age. Fingerprints allow identifying an individual even if he denies it, changes his name or appearance.

Moreno González ordered Doctor Eduardo González Mata, expert in fingerprint identification, to compare the fingerprints that were taken from the person allegedly named Mario Aburto Martínez at the offices of the Attorney General in Tijuana, on March 23rd, 1994, to those taken in Almoloya, on March 28th and 29th, 1994, from the person who said to be Mario Aburto Martínez.

Dr. González Mata presented his opinion on March 30th, 1994. His conclusion was:

"After performing the fingerprint study of the three ten-fingerprint records taken from Mr. Mario Aburto Martínez, it appears that according to the Vucetich System the three fingerprint records correspond in Dactyloscopic Formula or Individually, and that the dactylograms of the right thumb of each of the ten-fingerprint records correspond to the Fundamental Whorl Type (Extrodelto) and show thirteen Characteristic Points that coincide in position and form. Due to the aforementioned, the three ten-fingerprint records in question were printed by the same person."

* * *

Alphonse Bertillon, member of the Paris police since 1880, developed a criminal identification system known as anthropometry or Bertillon system, based on the fact that the body of every human being shows unrepeatable measurements and relationships.

The precision, accuracy and reliability of identification through fingerprints relegated the Bertillón system to the background, but it continues to be somehow useful.

Moreno González commissioned identification experts María de Lourdes Martínez Badillo and Jesús Agustín Luy Quijada to study Aburto's photographs taken at Lomas Taurinas and those taken at Almoloya, in order to determine if it was the same person.

The experts submitted their opinion on April 25th, 1994, concluding that the photographs show similar elements in the pinnal and nasal regions, chin, and facial pigmentation, allowing them to establish that the photographic images belong to the same person.

* * *

Once again, reiteratively, Montes asked identification expert, Ismael Hernández Montero to examine the photographs of the bloodstained Aburto from Lomas Taurinas, and to determine if his physiognomic features corresponded to Aburto, the prisoner.

The expert concluded that the physiognomic characteristics were identical, and observed that:

1. The forehead of the bloodstained individual is medium high and small in width, the same characteristics of the forehead of Mario Aburto Martínez.

2. The bloodstained individual has slightly arched, bushy and separated eyebrows, which are the same characteristics the eyebrows of Mario Aburto Martínez have.

3. The eyes of the bloodstained individual are closed, and in this position they are perceived as small in size. This layout is the same that Mario Aburto Martínez has with his eyes closed.

4. The nose of the bloodstained individual is medium-sized and rectilinear, which are the same features of the nose of Mario Aburto Martínez.

5. The nasobuccal space of the bloodstained individual is medium-sized, like the nasobuccal space of Mario Aburto Martínez.

6. The mixed type lips of the bloodstained individual have the same form, shape and those of Mario Aburto Martínez.

7. The mouth wrinkles of the bloodstained individual have the same characteristics as Mario Aburto Martínez.

8. The absence of hairiness in the nasobuccal grove on the bloodstained individual is the same as Mario Aburto Martínez.

9. The chin of the bloodstained individual, even though he is being grasped by the neck, is square in shape, Mario Aburto Martínez has the same shape.

10. The left ear of the bloodstained individual has the same

shape and dimensions as the left ear of Mario Aburto Martínez.

11. The shape of the hairline on the right zygomatic region of the bloodstained individual is the same as that of Mario Aburto Martínez.

12. The size of the navel and the plump waist, as well as the lack of hair on the chest and abdomen of the bloodstained individual are the same characteristics Mario Aburto Martínez has.

13. The slightly protruding cheekbones of the bloodstained individual have the same characteristics as those of Mario Aburto Martínez.

* * *

They had the chance to resort, once again to Dactylography. Moreno González appointed Doctor Luis Rives Galicia and expert photographer Petronilo Reyes Durán to study the fingerprints that appear in the admission record to the Federal Penitentiary Center of Almoloya, for intern Mario Aburto Martínez, as well as his National Military Service Record and voter's card, in order to determine if they belonged to the same person.

The experts' conclusion was that: "The three fingerprints under study belong to the same fundamental type of whorl in the Vucetich system, coinciding also in the same minutiae that individualize them in shape, size and location; therefore, we can state that the three fingerprints were printed by the right thumb of Mario Aburto Martínez, the name that appears in the documents in question."

* * *

Around midnight on March 23rd, 1994, María Luisa Martínez Piñones, Aburto's mother, visited him at the Attorney General's Office in Tijuana. She addressed him reproaching his behavior. "Tell me why you did it. Tell me the truth." Aburto was silent.

One month after the murder, Aburto's mother went to Almoloya to see her son again. She was very happy when she left because she saw "he was fatter, plum-cheeked, well dressed and clean." It is clear that the newspapers had failed to convince her of the two Aburtos theory.

* * *

Journalist Jesús Blancornelas, Director of the ZETA of Tijuana newspaper, decided to solve the problem of the two Aburtos in a different manner. Asking Aburto.

He put at stake all the relationships he had been able to form during a lifetime in journalism and obtained and exclusive interview. He was the only journalist that was able to interview Aburto. He traveled from Tijuana to Almoloya and entered the prison on Sunday, April 24th, 1994.

Almoloya was one of the first high-security prisons built in Mexico. It is surrounded by a closely monitored thick concrete wall. In order to cross it, the visitor must comply with very stringent identification procedures; he must hand in his tie, belt, pens, briefcases, papers and anything that the guards consider dangerous. Next comes a thorough body search. If after over an hour of paperwork the visitor gets through that first barrier, it will be only to face a second wall and more procedures. Only then he can go in. From that moment on, he will walk slowly through locks. Before him a door opens that closes behind him afterwards, leaving him in a space where he can neither advance nor retreat. A guard behind a bullet proof glass verifies his identity and, when he's satisfied, he operates the controls that will let him leave the lock and continue his way… up to the next lock.

Little by little, the cold of the prison penetrates the visitor. They say that prisoners sleep with fleece jackets, trying, unsuccessfully, to protect themselves from the freezing cold.

The guards accompanied Blancornelas up to meeting room number 2 where, behind a shatterproof glass, 23-year-old Aburto, was waiting for him. Aburto's voice went through the small holes in the glass to be recorded.

"Why do other people, for example, drug dealers or the same "Negro" Durazo or Portillo, why are they not punished?...

I accepted my responsibilities from the first moment of the accident, I said I am responsible for that accident and as such I want to pay, but true justice should be done, sir...

So many men. Echeverría as well, the killing he did in 68, has there even been justice for that as well? But in my case, see what they want to do with me. There has been talk about 30, 40, 50 years and to me that is not justice, sir."

Raskólnikov, the character of Dostoyevski's Crime and Punishment, was 23 when he killed an old usurer and her sister with an ax. After that he wondered, as Aburto did, why were there two rules and two measures? Why was Raskólnikov not been measured with the same yardstick as Napoleon? "No, those guys are not made of this stuff, the true *ruler*, the one who is permitted everything, bombards Toulon, plagues Paris, *forgets* his army in Egypt, *wastes* half a million soldiers in the retreat from Moscow and gets out of trouble with a pun in Vilnius; and yet, after death, statues are erected to him... Apparently, he was allowed everything."

Blancornelas returned Aburto to the questions he had prepared for him. "Our only interest is to talk with you for a moment. It has no other purpose, and we come for nothing else. And the first step we want to take is that us, in Zeta, this picture was taken when you were arrested (at Lomas Taurinas), and we just want you to tell us if this is you (he shows the picture)."

Aburto said: "Yes, sir. It's me."

On July 17th, 1928, on the pretext of making a pencil portrait, José de León Toral approached General Álvaro Obregón, president reelect of Mexico, who was attending the banquet that the Guanajuato council offered him at La Bombilla restaurant in San Ángel, Mexico City, and fired his concealed pistol, killing him. He always declared that he had acted on his own initiative.

Prosecuted and sentenced, he was executed on February 9th, 1929. He was 29 years old.

THE BOOK OF RECORDS

A few days after his appointment as special prosecutor, the Attorney General's Office provided Montes and his team with adequate offices to carry out their work. A small building located on the west side of Avenida de los Insurgentes, about two hundred meters south of the Viaducto.

There, Mario Crosswell Arenas examined hundreds of witnesses, and a team of experts, directed by Rafael Moreno González issued opinions on Psychology, Graphoscopy, the study of the conceptual content of documents, Psychiatry, Criminology, people movement, the victim – victimizer position, Topography, Criminalistics, etc.

Among many other elements that were established precisely, it became clear that Aburto had victimized Colosio by shooting twice a Taurus brand .38 special revolver, registration number 958400, model D-82, manufactured in Brazil. It was an old weapon, with chambers for six cartridges. However, it had only four cartridges, only two of which had been shot. The two that remained appeared to be very old and with a high possibility of failure.

*   *   *

General Domiro García was talking with Montes and his team. His face reflected the tragedy he was living. He had been entrusted with the safety of the candidate who had been killed in front of him. "Colosio made his protection very difficult", he alleged "he wanted to be in contact with the people." He explained, again and again, the right way to protect a celebrity: the diamond formation. The person whose security is involved moves in the middle of the protected area; around him as if positioned at the points of a star, are his guards, who protect him in this way from an attack coming from any direction. But of course, there was no barrier or diamond formation in Lomas Taurinas, only chaos, and a crowd advancing and pushing, on rough terrain with a steep slope.

That night I was watching a TV newscast that reported some of the acts of President Salinas' agenda. The screen showed the President walking through a carefully formed human corridor. Around him, as if placed at the points of a star, his guards observed a flawless diamond formation.

I felt the satisfaction we experience when we learn something new. Suddenly, the screen showed an indigenous woman, wearing sandals and a shawl, who, passing under the human barrier, ran to meet the President. The guards, surprised, moved to stop her. One of them took his right hand to the weapon he harbored in his armpit. But it was too late; she reached Salinas and called his attention by pulling his coat. Salinas, surprised, turned around. From the folds of her shawl she took out a flower and offered it to the President. He smiled and accepted the flower. The happy woman crossed the fence again and disappeared into the crowd.

I had just learned something else: the diamond formation is useless. If someone is willing to pay the price, he can kill anyone.

* * *

On March 23rd, 1994, at 22:30 hours, Elías Herrera Cruz was at home in the city of Tijuana, when a girl, whom he knew as Aburto's sister, appeared and told him that her mother, María Luisa Martínez Piñones, wanted him to go quickly to her home. He went in his car to Aburto's mother's home and she asked him to keep some of her son's papers that were important to him. Then, Aburto's mother brought out a tin chest, painted in green, padlocked, which they put in Herrera's car and he returned home. Minutes later María Luisa Martínez arrived with a grey book with red stripes with the word "Actas" (Records) printed on the cover, and a pair of glasses in its case. She opened the lock of the chest, introduced those objects, closed the chest again and said goodbye saying, "I'm leaving, good evening, I have to go because my son committed an atrocity, he shot someone, he is on TV right now, well I'm leaving" and she left.

Herrera learned what had happened that same day and, when he related the name Aburto Martínez to his neighbor and the chest he was keeping, he was afraid and went to the Municipal Police. The police took the chest and informed the Federal Prosecutor.

* * *

The book of Records was a notebook where Aburto had handwritten barely a dozen pages. But apparently, no one had read them. I got a copy to study it calmly in the silence of my library. The author's spelling was terrible. He ignored the use of the letter "h" (*istoria, erir, proivida, higual*), he mixed up "b" and "v" (*en vusca, deven*), "c" and "s" (*asiendoles, asepto, pasifista*), "m" and "n" (*inperio*). Accents, of course, were absent. Aburto affirmed himself as the "*eldest son of the homeland*". But if the spelling provoked laughter, the content shocked me.

Aburto clearly announced that he would kill the PRI candidate for the Presidency of the Republic, and he even stated when and where he would act: when the PRI reaches 65 years in power, where the country begins.

I talked to Montes on the telephone. I informed him about what I had found. The phrase "where the country begins" referred to Tijuana, but when would the PRI celebrate its 65th anniversary in power? Montes told me: Plutarco Elías Calles had founded the National Revolution Party (PNR) in 1929. The PRI turned 65 in 1994.

I talked to Montes another couple of times that afternoon. He instructed me to carefully study Aburto's pages, and to submit a written report. This is the final result of that study:

"MARIO ABURTO'S THOUGHTS"

"Mario Aburto Martínez is, undoubtedly, Mr. Luis Donaldo Colosio's murderer. However, public opinion still asks itself if Aburto has accomplices, if he premeditated the crime and which could be the reason for his action. If someone knows the *answer* to those questions it is without any doubt, Aburto himself. That is why, a Senator suggested having him examined under hypnosis, someone else asked to put him under the effects of Sodium Pentothal, and someone else has even demanded to torture him to get the truth out of him".

"However, not only Mexican Law forbids the Investigator from using these resources, but they are also useless. Indeed, Aburto, before committing the crime, developed an action project, which he recorded in a 14-page text, which he transcribed in a book of records. After the murder, Aburto used the pen again to write a few more pages."

"The careful reading of these texts gives us the information we seek. Aburto acted alone, premeditated his crime, and attributed a political meaning to his act."

"Therefore, we should listen carefully to Aburto. For such purpose, we transcribe, without comments, some of the paragraphs written by him. His spelling is not respected, since it would be very difficult to verify that his many errors have been reproduced, moreover it is useless for the purpose of this work."

"Our only involvement is to put paragraphs together by subject, which are separated in Aburto's text, and to direct the reader's attention by means of questions that are answered by Aburto's texts."

"I.- WHO DOES ABURTO IDENTIFY AS HIS ENEMY?"

> b) "Letting you know that in this country a party has formed an empire, that has deceived the people for many years, and that

uses the wrong terms which are not theirs, hiding also behind the great figures of the great Heroes of the Revolution."

b) "Even if you do not believe it, peoples and nations of the world, there are still dictators in this country, supported by the empire formed by a political party."

c) "That the working class be supported in its determined resistance to the imperialist plans of a party that has already been 65 years in power, because imperialism is endangering the fate of the country and of the whole nation."

"II.- WHICH ARE THE ENEMY'S SINS?"

b) "Those who are against the decisions of the people who are considered traitors."

b) "Because we perfectly know that there has been fraud in the elections and, therefore, the people ask international organizations, human rights defenders to be present in the country in order to enforce the people's decisions."

c) "At the same time two political parties will try to divide the power between them, who will join together in a desperate attempt to keep the power of the empire."

d) "Many people with positive ideas were executed by the empire, because they represented a threat to their Empire, and they knew that if they took away the blindfold from the people, without any doubt, their Empire would collapse."

e) "The current government has no ideas, and even less ideals, that could gain the trust of all the people. Hence it resorts to endless frauds."

"III.- WHO IS THE PERSON WHO INCARNATES THE ENEMY?"

b) "Its own Presidential candidate once admitted that his party had failed, and always spoke with demagoguery."

b) "The candidates truly elected by the people will be called to play their part."

c) "That is why the Presidential candidates must analyze well the responsibility in their hands."

d) "The campaign promises and petitions of any candidate, for any level post, should be signed by him and submitted to the public opinion and to the people across the entire Nation to be reviewed, accepted or rejected."

"IV.- WHO WILL SAVE THE COUNTRY?

b) "A son of the Fatherland. Eagle Knight. (signed by Mario Aburto Martínez)."

b) "He told me:

""Are you sure of what you say and your ideals? Because I agree with them."

"I answered yes."

"He said:"
"May it be for the good of the Fatherland and in the name of the people, I appoint you Eagle Knight."

"To which I replied:"

"I affirm without any reserve to keep and enforce the Constitution and the decisions of the people that are our country with its reforms to laws and patriotically carry out my appointment, watching for the good and prosperity of our country."

"To which he said:"

"If thou doest so, that the Nation may reward you, and if not it may require you."

c) "There will be much talk about the mission of the eldest son of the Fatherland and his deed that will change the course of history."

d) "History has been made by heroes, the great personalities, who have been followed by the crowd."

"V.- HOW WILL ABURTO SAVE THE COUNTRY?"

> b) "The true children of the Fatherland prove it with deeds, not words."

b) "The rulers who do not account to the people, with true justice and democracy, should pay for the consequences."

c) "Brothers, we must know what we want; when we want something we need to have the courage to say so; and when we say it, it is necessary to have the courage to do so."

d) "He who ensures that democracy be respected where it is not, is more useful to humanity than thousands of politicians together."

e) "We will force change through facts, not words, the people only believe in deeds, not words."

f) "Therefore, I reiterate that when you have the courage to say something, it is necessary to do it."

"VI.- WHAT PRICE WILL ABURTO PAY FOR SAVING THE NATION?"

> b) "Giving way to the ideals of a man who, concerned about the future of his country, decides to help to continue building a better country every day, at the cost of his own life, giving up everything, even his own family."

b) "And a true son of the Fatherland has to give up everything, only to serve the Nation, the people and its ideals."

"VII.- WHAT WILL ABURTO DO AFTER HIS HEROIC ACT?"

    b) "My statements will travel the world in search for support and understanding from the entire Latin American brother countries and from other continents."

    b) "That this book of records be reproduced by all the universities and be sold in the nation and around the world."

    c) "For such reason, I want to expose to public opinion a list of demands, and very soon I will make known why the facts that up to … have occurred."

"VIII.- WHERE WILL ABURTO ACT?"

"The change will be seen where the country begins."

"IX.-WHEN WILL ABURTO ACT?"

"We intend to free the nation… from the Empire that has failed, just when it reaches 65 years in power…"

"X.- WHO IS RESPONSIBLE FOR THE ACTS PERFORMED BY ABURTO?"

    b)   "May all those rulers who always wanted to make decisions that corresponded only to the people be responsible for the facts."

    b)   "May all bad rulers, who failed to comply with true justice and democracy be responsible for all the events …"

"XI.- BEFORE MR. COLOSIO, DID ABURTO CONSIDER ANY OTHER POSSIBLE VICTIM?"

"I have been working for eight years on a project to have a country that is better every day. I remember when I had been working on the project for only one year that it nearly cost me my life because I revealed it to a follower of the Empire. I was only seventeen years old, and maybe for that reason, they did not take it seriously…"

He was one of those individuals who stays silent in order not to make noise. Regular loser of so many battles won by oblivion. He never gave the slightest cause for alarm, Commissioner. Nobody imagined that he was hiding a gun in the closet.

Citizen Zero, what obscure reason made you come out of the hole?

He loaded the shotgun. He put on his jacket thinking about the pictures.

He did not have and evil eye, seventeen dead in thirty shots.

When he was put in the police car, finally arrested: "Now, he said all Spain shall know my two surnames."

Joaquín Sabina.

ABURTO

Mario Aburto Martínez was born in La Rinconada, Michoacán, on October 3rd, 1970. He is the second of six children: Rafael, who was 24 in 1994; Mario, 23; Rubén, 22; José Luis, 20; Elizabeth, 16 and Karina, 10 years old, children of María Luisa Martínez Piñones and Rubén Aburto Cortés.

Three years before Aburto's birth, on September 16th, 1967, his father, a conflictive, loud and violent man, in a drunken state of inebriation, had killed his brother Raúl Aburto Cortés and J. Cruz Ventura Ortiz. The murderer, Rubén Aburto Cortés was 23 years old. He immediately fled and the arrest warrant issued against him for the double homicide could not be executed.

The fact that the parent of the family had to live from hand to mouth, forced the family to frequently change address. From 1972 to 1974, Rubén went to the United States, abandoning his family who took refuge at the parental grandparents' home in Zacapu, Michoacán. In 1975, Rubén returned from the United States and took his family to Mexico City, to live in the Progreso Nacional neighborhood. Their stay in the capital city was less than a year long, because Rubén did not like the city and decided to return to La Rinconada. Mario continued his studies there until he got his certificate for secondary education on June 30th, 1986. That would be the end of his studies.

In 1987, given the precarious economic situation of the family, Mario Aburto went to live with his uncle Manuel, in Ciudad Lázaro Cárdenas. Manuel's wife, Avelina, wanted Mario Aburto to study in that city, but Mario decided that his brother should rather go to school while he worked. The stay in Lázaro Cárdenas did not last more than one year. In early 1988, the father, Rubén Aburto, decides to permanently move to the United States. Then, the family abandons La Rinconada, for the last time, to move to Tijuana, in order to be closer to the father.

Mario Aburto arrives in Tijuana in March 1988. His brother, Rafael, spoke to the manager of the lumberyard "Las Californias", where he worked, asking him to give his brother a job. He did not accept, since he did not have any vacant positions, but allowed him to stay in the lumberyard, in a half-built wooden room, which furniture was a bed and a desk.

The third week of March 1989, considering his father's will, Mario Aburto moved to the United States to work. His brothers Rubén and Rafael Aburto Martínez also traveled to that country for the same purpose. The mother, María Luisa remained in Tijuana with the other members of the family: José Luis, Elizabeth and Karina, and Patricia Ochoa Vega, Rafael's wife.

Mario's stay in the United States was short, in December 1990 he returned to Mexico since the family was concerned that María Luisa and her three young children were unprotected. Together they decided that Mario should come back, since he was the most responsible.

During his stay in the United States, Mario worked at Geron Furniture, Inc. and sent his mother money to buy a lot of land. On January 11th, 1990, María Luisa buys lot 1596, located in block number 9, second urban section (Mexicali 20842), colonia Buenos Aires Norte, ejido Chilpancingo. The family considered that the property belonged to Mario, since he contributed most of the money. There they built two brick rooms, with a wooden roof and cement floor. At the back of the lot a small room with a septic tank was built from board and wood. The family was poor.

Mario is a lonely, introverted, friendless, serious, reserved, respectful individual. He is always angry, upset at society, at his circumstances, even at himself. He cares a lot about his appearance. He wore simple clothes, but he was always clean and tidy, he did not smoke, nor did he consume alcohol or drugs. He stood with his chest out, head steady, right up, without moving it, without turning, chin up. His stare was as if other people did not exist, as if he believed he was superior to others, as if no one deserved him.

He wanted to excel economically, to help his family out of the poverty in which they lived. But his desire to excel was frustrated because he was not qualified to fill the position to which he aspired.

Since he returned to Tijuana, in December 1990, until March 23rd, 1994, Aburto worked in six or seven different companies, always for short periods of time, sometimes a few days. He would leave the job claiming he did not like it or that the salary was very low. Sometimes he would not even collect the remuneration for the days worked.

On January 25th, 1994 Aburto appeared at the company Camero Magnéticos, S.A. de C.V., which had published an advertisement in "El Mexicano" newspaper for a job for mechanics specialized in injection machines. He was received by the plant manager, José Enrique Rodarte Chaparro, who gave him the relevant exam, on basic electricity notions, industrial electricity and molding and hydraulics knowledge. Aburto failed. What the company needed were electro-mechanical engineering interns, and Aburto had barely finished secondary school. But at Aburto's insistence to be hired, Rodarte spoke with Engineer David Pérez, responsible for Audiomático, S.A. de C.V. (a subsidiary factory of Camero Magnéticos) and he hired him.

Aburto began working as maintenance assistant at Audiomático on February 7th, 1994, in the morning shift, from 6:00 am to 2:00 pm. Martín Vélez was in charge of training him in the use of the magnetic tape cutting machine.

* * *

Alma Rosa Cruz Soto was born on March 8th, 1977, in Mazatlán, Sinaloa. In early 1994, her parents sent her to Tijuana to live with her uncle Guillermo Salazar Medina and aunt Lourdes Beatriz Rodríguez López. Alma Rosa was 16, but her physical appearance and behavior made her look like a girl. Her aunt worked at Camero Magnéticos, and managed to get her niece to work there as well. Alma Rosa started working on January 24th, 1994, as an assembler in the first shift, from 6:00 am to 14:00 pm.

She met Aburto there, they both took the company's bus to work, Mario invited her to visit the planisphere and they agreed to meet on February 8th at 3:00 o'clock at the planisphere door, to make the most out of Alma Rosa's day off. They both showed up for the appointment, but Mario suggested visiting the Tijuana dam instead. At the dam, Aburto told her about his family: that his mother was living with him, but that he did not know where his dad was. Then he told her he was a politician and was going to kill Colosio, strongly emphasizing that she should not tell anybody. Alma Rosa said, "Don't do it". But Mario insisted "I am going to do it alone and I will make them pay you more", referring to the workers. Then, Aburto said, "I am going to write a book in order to become famous." Alma Rosa said, "If you're going to write a book in order to be famous, then why are you going to kill Colosio?" Aburto remained silent.

On March 10th, Alma Rosa's parents aware that she was going out with Aburto, went to Tijuana and took her back to Mazatlán.

On March 23rd, 1994, Alma Rosa was having dinner with her family and watching TV. The program was interrupted to break the news of the attack in Tijuana. When she saw the news she was shocked. That night she slept very poorly. Her father, her mother and her two sisters, had the TV on all night to watch the news. That affected her, she was scared because Mario Aburto had told her he was going to kill Colosio and she did nothing to report it to the authorities. She thought that if she had denounced him, she could have prevented the murder.

* * *

Graciela González Díaz started working in Camero Magnéticos on March 9th, 1994, she was 16 years old. She was assigned to a workstation close to Aburto, so she met him the same day. The next day Alma Rosa left Tijuana. Aburto immediately invited Graciela on a date and they went out on March 12th. They went to the wax museum. The figure of an Aztec warrior is near the museum door. Aburto told her that it was an eagle knight and said, "When you go back to Tijuana, you will see me represented in a wax figure". Then he invited her to eat at a Chinese restaurant. He told her that he could handle firearms and if she wished to, he would teach her. He also told her he had been living in the United State, where his father lived and that he attended a shooting club in that country. He also told her that he was writing a book in which he captured his political ideas and that someday his book would be published.

* * *

José Juan Quintero Téllez worked as Plant Manager at Camero Magnéticos. Enrique Rodarte assigned Aburto to work under his orders. He commissioned him with cleaning the machines. On March 15th, Aburto approached him asking if he could borrow a tool to disassemble a set of knives, since the tape running inside the machine was tangled up and the machine was not working. Quintero saw what had happened and verified that Aburto had caused the breakdown of four blades that are installed in two cylinders, which had caused the magnetic tapes to tangle up. He immediately ordered Aburto not to touch the machine. The damage that he had caused was substantial. Quintero calculated it was worth around US$25,000 and the replacement blades had to be imported from Germany. It was obvious that Aburto was not trained.

* * *

Marcelino Ortíz Martínez and Mauricio Ortíz Martínez, both Aburto's cousins, also worked for Camero Magnéticos. On March 17th, 1994 Aburto invited them to his house where he showed them a gun he took out from under his bed mattress. He showed it to them for several minutes while he told them he was planning to do some business on the 22nd or 23rd of March.

The two cousins noted Aburto was extremely nervous.

* * *

María Elena Lugo Valdés started working at Audiomático on March 10th, 1994. She met Aburto there. On March 18th, he approached the machine where María Elena was working and began talking to her. He was very angry because the machine he was working on had broken down. "It breaks down very often", he said, since they didn't fix it correctly and then they blamed him. Now the knives had fallen off. He asked María Elena about her family, how many children she had. María Elena told him she had two children, aged two and three. Aburto was silent for a while, thoughtful, and then he said he was leaving the factory, because he was going to make more money at the job he had before, in politics. He was going to do something very important. He would risk his life. María Elena asked him what he would do: are you going to rob a bank or kill someone? Aburto answered that María Elena would see on TV what he would do between March 23rd and 25th. That he was going to risk his life for the country in order to change it, that workers were abused, that they were paid very little.

* * *

Daniel Pineda Vázquez worked at Camero Magnéticos as assistant supervisor. He met Aburto, but had a superficial relationship with him, since they only saw each other at work sometimes, when they put their personal belongings in the lockers that were near the injection machines, he also got to see him in the company's bus going downtown. He realized that Aburto was a lonely person who had no friends. He recalls that on March 23rd, he approached Aburto's work place, noticing that there was a calendar on the wall where all the week of March 15th through 24th was marked in pen. The 23rd and the 24th were crossed out.

* * *

On March 23rd, 1994, Aburto worked his shift normally. He entered the company at 5:54 am and ended his working day at 13:59 hours.

When he and a group of peers were coming down from the dining room to return to work at 10:30, he addressed his colleague Pedro Silva Solórzano in a loud voice and said: "Master, today is the day, today I will be famous!"

After finishing work, he asked Tomás Hernández Mendoza, in charge of access and exit control of the factory, where the Lomas Taurinas neighborhood was and which was the best way to get there. Hernández Mendoza made a mistake since, at that time, there were many employees going in and out of the company, because it was time to change shifts, and gave him directions to get to Colonia Panamericana. Aburto thanked him and boarded the yellow minibus carrying workers downtown. He asked the driver, José García Martínez, where Lomas Taurinas was. He sat next to Olivia Moreno López, a coworker from the same shift. Aburto was wearing a black shirt and jacket. During the trip they commented about Alma Rosa Cruz Soto. Aburto got off downtown, which was unusual, since he always got off at the corner of 5th and 10th streets. He ran across Constitución street and continued running through third street, heading for Niños Héroes.

Aburto ate a sandwich and drank a soda along the way. Asking around, he managed to board a bus with the words "Lomas Taurinas" on the windshield.

Aburto arrived at Lomas Taurinas between 15:40 and 15:50. When Colosio arrived, Aburto was already waiting.

* * *

On July 1st, 1994, a hearing in the trial against Aburto was held. Almoloya was initially intended to be a prison solely for sentenced inmates. Therefore, it had no premises for courts. Later on, it housed defendants, such as Aburto, and it was necessary to improvise premises so that hearings could be held. Federal judges of the State of Mexico, who knew these procedures, left their offices, located in Toluca, and moved, together with all the court personnel, their machines and files, to Almoloya so that the procedure could take place in the uncomfortable conditions of the improvised premises.

The Attorney General, i.e., the Public Prosecutor, was represented by Marco Antonio Díaz de León. I attended as special advisor to the prosecutor. Marco Antonio had been a Public Prosecutor for several years, besides being a university professor and author of numerous books on criminal proceedings. In 1994, he was Chief of Staff of the Attorney General and no longer went to court to manage the processes directly. But this was a special case, and the Attorney General had asked Díaz de León to come to the trenches once again.

Waiting for the hearing to start, Díaz de León and I talked with Judge Alejandro Sosa Ortíz. We addressed each other with all the courtesy of our profession. The Judge called us "Doctor Díaz de León" and "Doctor Zamora Pierce", and we respectfully called him "Your Honor". Aburto, seating a short distance from us, followed our conversation attentively.

The purpose of the hearing was to extend Aburto's statement. Once it started, he stood up and addressed the judge calling him "Your Honor", and saying "I respectfully request Your Honor to be allowed to extend my statement without interruptions, since otherwise it would be limiting my defense and I think it would distort the essence of this hearing, because everything I will mention is part of the extension of my statement which has true facts and I also request once again that, due to judicial economy, not to be interrupted."

He was speaking following some notes he carried with him. He cited article 250 of the Federal Code of Criminal Procedures, according to which statements shall be drawn using in as much as possible the same words used by the deponent, but he asked the Judge not to be judged "for using some terminology that might be wrong since then I would be judged for my ignorance and lack of culture, taking into account the knowledge and education of those who depose against me, because they are educated people with a career, therefore some words that I have mentioned should not be taken into account to be used against me, because I do not know much about the terminology, so I will try to conduct myself as best as I can so there can be a better understanding between the parties in the process... because I wanted to study to make my family proud, since there are no professionals with a college degree in my family and due to economic problems I could not continue my studies. Then I thought about joining the army so that my friends, my family and the Nation would be proud of me, but I gave up joining the army because I did not like weapons or chasing crooks, since my goal was to study economics and get a PhD,"

Listening to Aburto I thought, first, that he was reproaching both Díaz de León and myself. "I could also be a Doctor", he told us, "but I couldn't because I'm poor". After a few minutes I wondered if Aburto knew that Colosio had studied economics in the Instituto Tecnológico de Monterrey and had done postgraduate studies at the University of Pennsylvania and Vienna.

Aburto continued talking for hours, it was evident he was enjoying the moment intensely. He talked and the rest of us listened, a clerk was taking notes of each and every one of his words. He was standing and the others were seating. He was the star. Whatever he said would be reported in the newspapers the next day. He was a man who had reached his goal.

During the three months since the murder, several hearings had taken place in the process. There, Aburto had heard the judge's, the prosecutor's, the clerks' and the lawyers' statements. He had learned their terminology and their way of speaking, and now he imitated them incorrectly. It was a parody, in which Aburto stated the defense arguments that he had managed to sketch: the Book of Records should not be used as evidence against him, because articles 6 and 7 of the Constitution grant freedom of expression, freedom to write and publish; he had only wounded Colosio, who had entered the hospital alive, "making it possible to think that he could also have died, perhaps due to a badly performed surgery, due, perhaps to the nervousness of the doctor..."

* * *

On September 16th, 1994, at Aburto's request, the reconstruction of events took place in Almoloya, directed by Aburto himself. The fourth special prosecutor, Luis Raúl González Pérez, comments the video of the reconstruction as follows:

"The reconstruction of the events lasts one hour, which displays his histrionics. He focuses the attention of others to himself, shows the qualities he believes to have, regarding stage direction, actors presentation, lighting management, trying to appear as an expert.

He manages the actors (men) who support the reconstruction, he gradually increases the atmosphere of his performance; he first asks a man to help him, then he replaces him because he has not the height he needs (the requirements to be part of his cast). His need of widely showing his qualities as director require him to ask for other people in the scene, whom he can manipulate (*"raise your arm, move your leg, put the gun in your waist band, etc."*). He asks the photographer (*"make this shoot, another one here on the leg, another one that shows the gun"*).

Mario, rather than defending himself against the fact of being a murderer, shows all his grandeur, his apparent wisdom, he feels unique, the capturing everybody's attention, he is different, he is outstanding.

From that momentarily elevated position, he has the gift to disqualify anyone who could compete with him, since he assumes himself as an expert in almost any field. With the experts from the PGR and other experts, *"experts on the subject never make a reconstruction of events as I'm doing here but, for some reason, they try to hide truth, you could say reconstruction as it could have been, why? We do not know, we do not know the truth, possibly as I have mentioned, it could have been done by someone in the Security staff that was unaware, that was new in the job, or who possibly had no knowledge of weapons and had never been in a meeting.* And he added that these are *"the contradictions that are allegedly experts in the field."*

He sharply remarked that the technical conditions were not

suitable for his video recording (*"that is why experts in filming use highly complete lighting, in order to avoid such errors, that is why they use reflectors and I believe that even a very small person ‹he turns toward the camera man›, may realize that that is true"*).

His narcissism subordinates his histrionic behaviors and he even issues psychological interpretations as a great expert (*"when you are angry against someone, or some feeling, criminals discharge the full gun and, in the first place, you can see that the shot, the movements that I did, feet, body movements, I had no intention to harm the person whom I did not know who he was"*).

His rebellion against authority also appears quickly and thoughtlessly (at the end of Mario's statement-performance, the judge said: "we understand that this diligence is over", to which Mario immediately responds NO."

No. Aburto did not want to have the reconstruction of events finished. He didn't want to end the criminal proceeding against him. Citizen zero did not want to go back to his hole.

On September 6th, 1901, the President of the United States, William Mckinley, attended the Pan-American Exposition, which took place in Buffalo, Nueva York. Someone approached him. Believing it was a fan, Mckinley extended his hand to greet him. He was actually the anarchist Leon Czolgosz, who shot two shoots point-blank that, a few days later, resulted in death.

Czolgosz, who was 29 years old, was sentenced to death and executed. His last words were: "I killed the President because he was the enemy of good people, good workers. I feel no remorse for my crime.".

THE CONSPIRACY

When Colosio finished speaking, Rodolfo Mayoral Esquer and others, tried to form a barrier for the candidate to leave Lomas Taurinas. But Colosio went down on the opposite side of the barrier in progress. Mayoral Esquer then struggled to stand in front of Colosio and, with his arms extended in front of him, tried to open the way. All of a sudden he heard two gunshots, he turned around to see what had happened and saw many people falling over each other. He came closer and saw that his father was one of the fallen and that other people were beating him. He helped him to his feet. He helped arresting Aburto and accompanied those who had arrested him to the truck where they transferred him. People prevented the vehicle from moving. Mayoral Esquer started running in front of the vehicle opening the way. When he saw that there were no people obstructing the way, he stepped aside to leave it free way. He then went down the hill and found someone known by the name of Cota, who offered to take him in his car. He asked if he had seen his father, Vicente Mayoral Valenzuela, and Cota replied "Don't worry, he must have left in another vehicle." They went to Hospital del Prado, thinking that Colosio had been taken there. When they heard on the radio the news that he had been taken to the General Hospital, they went there. Mayoral Esquer learned, from people's comments that his father had been arrested. He went then to the Attorney General's Office, where they refused to give him any information. So he took a taxi and headed for the PRI offices in the state, where he found

Rivapalacio and informed him about his father's arrest. At that time Tranquilino Sánchez arrived, after going home to change his clothes, because those he was wearing at Lomas Taurinas had got very dirty. Learning about the arrest of Mayoral Valenzuela he said, "Why has he been arrested if we both arrested Aburto? If necessary I can testify."

The next morning Mayoral Esquer went to the Attorney General's Office together with Rivapalacio and Tranquilino Sánchez. It was not necessary for Tranquilino to declare. The Attorney General had already informed the press that Mayoral Valenzuela would be released, and, in fact he was released at 22:00 hours.

* * *

José Rodolfo Rivapalacio Tinajero had been an active member of the PRI for 30 years. On the occasion of Colosio's visit to Tijuana, he was in charge of putting together a group of people who, voluntarily and free of charge, would form the barrier to allow the candidate's entry to and exit from Lomas Taurinas.

When the event finished at Lomas Taurinas, Rivapalacio left quickly to go to the Gran Hotel Tijuana, where the next event in the candidate's agenda would take place. When he reached the paved part of the street, Juan García Colín told him that it was being announced through his portable radio that gunshots had been heard. He immediately went back towards the wooden bridge and saw the vehicles carrying Colosio leaving. Later on, having learned that a helicopter had been requested from the US authorities to move Colosio to a hospital in the United States, he began monitoring the arrival of the helicopter. When it arrived, he entered the hospital up to where it was allowed, until he found Doctor Juan Medrano Padilla, whom he informed that the helicopter was already outside the hospital. The Doctor replied that given Colosio's serious condition, he didn't think the transfer would be authorized.

* * *

Raúl Loza Parra, Deputy Delegate of the Federal Judicial Police in the State of Baja California, commissioned Marco Antonio Jácome Saldaña and Gerardo Millán Leal to film the events of the PRI candidate in Tijuana. Both went first to the airport and then to Lomas Taurinas, where they looked for a suitable place to film the speech that Colosio would deliver and decided on a house that was on the right side, behind the platform. They asked the owner for permission and climbed to the roof to film. The roof was already full of photographers. In order to shoot without obstacles, Millán Leal climbed a wall and Jácome held him in precarious balance while he filmed the whole event.

Many other cameramen, from different news programs, filmed the act at Lomas Taurinas. But almost all of them considered their work finished when Colosio finished speaking and left the platform, so they stopped shooting. Jácome Saldaña and Millán Leal, however, continued filming. Their film records Colosio's difficult progress to exit Lomas Taurinas and the time when Aburto puts the revolver to his temple and shoots.

The television companies soon had a copy of this film and started broadcasting it, again and again. Some television commentators, projecting the film in slow motion, believed to identify, in the chaotic mass of Lomas Taurinas, some movements with a precise purpose. With a ruler in hand, as schoolteachers, they pointed at some guy that hindered Colosio's progress and another one that opened a space where Aburto stepped in. They concluded that Aburto had had accomplices. The murder was a result of a conspiracy.

Besides the film, the Attorney General had the testimony of Domiro Roberto García Reyes, who declared that Tranquilino Sánchez Venegas, a burly subject in a black jacket and cap with a white emblem and mustache, located himself behind Colosio, to his right and interfered abruptly and aggressively with García Reyes, preventing him from approaching the candidate the moment immediately prior to the first shot.

Finally, one of Aburto's coworkers, Graciela González Díaz, affirmed that she had seen Aburto talking with Tranquilino, on March 10th, 1994, at the Parque de la Amistad.

With these elements, the Attorney General's Office exercised criminal action against Tranquilino on March 28th, 1994 for the crime of homicide, before Montes took office, on that same date.

As soon as he took office, Montes found that there was evidence that allowed presuming the responsibility of others. The film showed that apparently Vicente Mayoral Valenzuela opened the way for a man who disappeared from the image when he was in front of Colosio. Had he thrown himself to the ground? Was he trying to stop Colosio's march? TV commentators baptized him as "The Diver".

Colonel Federico Antonio Reynaldos del Pozo, responsible for security, who was walking in front of Colosio, stated that Mayoral Esquer had pushed him.

And, of course, if there were reasons to suspect Tranquilino and the Mayorals, such suspicion involved Rodolfo Rivapalacio, who had asked them to form barriers, at no charge, at Lomas Taurinas.

If the Prosecution, knowing that evidence, had not brought criminal action, it would have failed in its duty, would have incurred in liability and could have been validly accused of being guilty of letting the accused avoid the action of justice.

Thus, the Attorney General's Office exercised criminal action against Vicente Mayoral Valenzuela, Rodolfo Mayoral Esquer and José Rodolfo Rivapalacio Tinajero on the charges of murder and conspiracy.

*　*　*

In their Court statements, the accused vigorously declared their innocence. Far from participating in the crime, Mayoral Valenzuela had disarmed Aburto and, together with Tranquilino, had participated in his arrest. They did not know Aburto and all they had done was to make way for Colosio. That was why they were spreading their arms, and pushing people.

In Almoloya, on March 25th, 1994, just a couple of days after the murder, Aburto, in his initial statement, aware that Tranquilino was also accused, stated, "that it is his wish not to have innocent people involved, such as the person who was arrested along with the respondent, and in that regard he has represented that he did not participate in the fact, and that neither his family was aware of what the respondent was going to perform and he also wants to reiterate that no innocent people should be involved… and also, because of what has been said, he does not seek his freedom, because he is aware of what he did."

On April 6th, 1994, in his preliminary statement on the new process on conspiracy with the Mayorals and Rivapalacio, that was filed, Aburto reiterated: "That all the persons are innocent, all those that are mentioned in the first video that was shown to me, where it is mentioned that there was a partnership, there was no collaboration…"

Thereafter, every time Aburto appeared in Court, he insisted that he did not know his co-defendants and that they were innocent. Aburto never showed pity for the man whose life he had destroyed, no remorse for his conduct. But he repeatedly defended the innocence of his co-defendants. Did he really pity them or did he only want to get these intruders out of the scenario where he was the only actor?

Through a court order dated April 10th, 1994, the Judge ordered the Rivapalacio's release, but the Mayorals were brought to trial, as well as Tranquilino by virtue of a previous court order.

* * *

In order to demonstrate the theory of a concerted action, the prosecution needed to prove that Aburto and his co-defendants had known each other previously, and that they had agreed to collaborate in committing the crime. The investigations did not provide any evidence of those facts. To the contrary, the hypothesis that Colosio had been killed by a lone murderer grew stronger every day.

The accusation against Tranquilino and the Mayorals was based, mainly, on the filming of what had happened at Lomas Taurinas. With the support of the Spanish Government Montes was helped by experts Ángel Luis Fernández Cobos, Head of Central Forensic Science in Spain, Juan López Palafox, Head of Criminal Investigation of the Central Service, and Ana Blanco Almendros, Expert in Forensic Documents.

These experts projected and viewed the disputed images dozens of times, they wrote a report with 102 photographs attached, which corresponded to frozen images of the videos that they had analyzed and they also enclosed pieces thereof, that show the characters whose movements were of interest, such as Aburto's, Tranquilino's and the Mayorals'. They also prepared graphs in which they pointed out, with color lines, the route that each of the characters in question had followed.

With scientific rigor, the experts pointed out that: "Photography, as an experts' element for comparison, must always be accompanied by metric witnesses and must be performed from different levels, in order to transform the two-dimensional image into its three-dimensional reality. Otherwise, it is difficult to determine if two individuals, apparently together are on the same plane, or, to the contrary, it is a simple optical effect, resulting from the photographic flattening." And they stated that the observed characters' movements are normal, considering the pressure from the people. The video does not allow to state, or deny, that Tranquilino voluntarily gave way to Aburto, since the protection group was overwhelmed by people. Vicente Mayoral makes no strange movements. Rodolfo Mayoral's positions are logical.

The fact that the murder was committed with a used revolver, which was first purchased in 1977, that because it was old it could have failed and that only 4 of the 6 chambers in the revolver were charged with old cartridges that could also fail, also spoke against a conspiracy. Aburto knew his gun was inadequate. During the days prior to the crime, he tried to acquire a better one, but he had no money and could not do it.

The accusation made by General Domiro Roberto García Reyes,

that Tranquilino had intercepted and pushed him on the day of the events, also collapsed, since when he testified before the Judge, on June 23rd, 1994, he acknowledged that he had been stopped by two short women who, coming from his right side, got between him and the candidate.

The man whom the TV presenters called "The Diver", because his head suddenly disappears from the image in the film, assuming that he had thrown himself to the ground in order to stop Colosio, was identified as Mario Alberto Carrillo Cuevas. He was a collaborator of Basilio Meza, Secretary of Electoral Action of the PRI in Tijuana. His boss instructed him to go to the airport to form a barrier for Colosio's arrival. He went from there, on his own initiative, to the meeting at Lomas Taurinas. At the end of the meeting, he was about 5 meters away from the truck that served as platform. He asked those near him to make a barrier so that the candidate could leave and he imitated a person he had seen at the airport who had tried to open the way for Colosio walking backwards with outstretched arms. He neither fell nor ducked. We need to assume that his head disappears from the film due to the uneven terrain. He heard an explosion and saw the candidate falling and then heard the second explosion. He saw Aburto throwing the gun and being stopped by several people. He grabbed Aburto by the hair and started beating him. He held Aburto's back and right arm and kept pounding him. He helped to lead Aburto to the suburban truck in which he was removed from Lomas Taurinas.

On May 30th, 1994, Rafael Moreno González, reported the results of the criminalistics services under his charge. In the report he states that Aburto acted alone. "Criminologists", he says, "coincide that assassins act alone, they commit the offense in public, do not resist arrest and accept having committed the crime. Regicides almost always meditate the preparation and performance of their act by themselves, not wanting to share the honor and merit with anyone. It has always been recognized that a regicide is, by his very nature, a loner, without accomplices or informers even in his most immediate intimacy."

In his report, Moreno González cites the diagnoses that were established, derived from Aburto's personality study:

"- Psychological.- Narcissistic and histrionic personality disorder.
- Psychiatrist.- Delusional disorder (paranoid).
- Criminology.- Low social adaptability, no apparent intimacy, high harm, high criminal capacity and high danger.
- Social work.-
- Family group: Modified, dysfunctional, disintegrated and disorganized extended family.
- Work area: Occupationally unstable.
- School area: Maladjustment and poor school achievement.
- Social environment: Lacking and with limitations.

These diagnoses, mainly the medical – psychiatric allow establishing that Mario Aburto Martínez did not need any concerted action to commit the crime he is charged with, and no one to motivate him."

* * *

The new elements revealed by the investigation oblige making a decision: should they be communicated to the judge or not? Some voices in the Attorney General's Office supported not doing it. Montes was blunt:

"I cannot accept an innocent man being in jail because I hid information that could have set him free." In his final report he said: "If we persisted in maintaining as true something that we now know has lost strength, just to defend an apparent consistency with an initial position, we would be driving the issue, in a blameworthy way, to a situation that would not allow the truth to be known. However, if we report what we now know, the path to true knowledge of what happened is leveled. If the new data lead to different judgments and rectify others taken, the prosecution will be fulfilling its ethical and legal duties."

Consequently, Montes instructed the Deputy Attorney of Process Control to provide the necessary evidence in the proceedings so the

Judge was informed about the newly obtained information.

One evening when we were chatting and drinking coffee, aware of the tremendous pressures weighting on Montes, I recalled that in an English provincial courtroom, a notice placed on one of the walls reported: "In this Court, the Crown always wins, because when an innocent person is acquitted, the Crown also wins".

Montes' decision allowed, sometime after, Tranquilino's and the Mayorals' acquittal.

* * *

Montes felt that his work was finished. He decided to report the results. First, to Colosio's widow, who had chosen him to head the investigation. Montes and the key members of his team went to Periférico Sur, to the house that Colosio had used as his campaign headquarters, where we had an appointment with Diana Laura. Extremely thin and pale, with obvious signs of the disease that was killing her, Diana Laura listened upset that the investigation pointed to a lone murderer. She did not want to hear any reasons or arguments. She wanted to be right: Colosio had been the victim of a conspiracy. That was Montes' last meeting with Diana Laura. A few days later, she hired the services of Juan Velázquez to represent her.

The next visit was to the Senate, to report. Porfirio Muñoz Ledo was waiting there for Montes. Both, as legislators, had had a confrontation in which Muñoz Ledo did not fare well. Now, spiteful, he attacked Montes' report with all his talent and irony. There was no room for reasoning in that environment, nor desire to find the truth. Politics is not the best environment to search for historical truth.

An old ailment attacked Montes again and forced him to use a cane. In this way, walking with difficulty, we arrived at Los Pinos. José Carreño Carlón led us to a room, furnished as a TV studio where we would film a report on the case. The makeup artist applied a bit of powder, "so we would not shine". The cameraman did a countdown: four, three, two, one... and we started recording. Montes presented the main results of the research, and I commented on the analysis of the Book of Records.

A few days later, Carreño Carlón informed us that the recording had been projected to small audiences, the overwhelming reaction was negative. People did not believe in the lone murderer hypothesis.

* * *

Montes informed the President that he was going to inform the public of the result of his investigations. Salinas asked him not to do it. The opinion surveys of the Presidency showed that 85% of the people believed there was a conspiracy behind Colosio's assassination.

Montes informed the press and all hell broke loose. The presidential candidates of the PAN, PRD, PT, PPS, PARM, PFCRN, PDM and PVEM indicated that the turnaround of the investigation was incredible, since the new hypothesis of Assistant Attorney General Montes was intended to fool the population and that made them fear the worst. Porfirio Muñoz Ledo said that Montes' report was an insult to intelligence. Legislators from different parties expressed their fears that such critical matter would be "shelved". The President of the Employers' Confederation of the Mexican Republic, Antonio Sánchez Díaz de Rivera, qualified Montes' statements as "a mockery to Mexican society." Members of Congress accused Montes of irresponsibility and ineptitude. The Catholic Church demanded the resignation of the prosecutor because the authorities did not want to get to the truth. Soon cartoonists joined the attack, using all the vitriol of their pens to ridicule Montes. Chubasco drew Montes, with a magnifying glass in his hand, saying "Colosio committed suicide!" Helioflores paints a stormy sea in which a ragged castaway floats on a buoy. The castaway is Montes and the buoy is, actually the top of a huge submerged question mark. The cartoon is entitled "Man alone." Naranjo shows us a police agent (coat, hat, sunglasses), identified because his hat said "Special Deputy Attorney General", who misses the fingerprints passing by his side. In fact, when we look closely, what seemed to be sunglasses, covering his eyes are actually some of those fingerprints. Helioflores presents Montes seating at a desk, under which, laying on the ground, is the record of the Colosio case. On top of the desk, before Montes, is his resignation. Montes, with the pen in his hand, says, "Almost, almost".

Public enemy number one was not Aburto anymore, it was Montes.

"I called my kids to meet at my house tonight, Montes told me in a pained voice, I want them to see that I'm still the same human being as always, and not the monster that has been drawn in the newspapers."

* * *

On July 1994, Montes resigned as Special Deputy Attorney General. He gave the President a final report in which he states:

"Mister President:

Having you appointed me as Special Assistant Attorney General of the Attorney General's Office for the investigation of the murder of Mr. Luis Donaldo Colosio Murrieta, I set myself the goal of knowing the historical truth, according to objective scientific criteria and in strict accordance to law.

For such purpose, I put together a work team of distinguished jurists and investigators. The so structured, Special Deputy Attorney General's Office got 312 statements from witnesses, produced 48 technical studies and collected 103 videos and 2040 photographs for analysis.

As a result of its work, the Special Office was able to fully prove, beyond reasonable doubt, that the material and intellectual author of the murder is Mario Aburto Martínez, who acted alone, premeditated his crime for long and attributes his action to political motivation… Logically, there will always be a possibility that new evidence may be known. I consider that there is a very low probability that this new evidence, should it exist, requires changing the conclusions reached today by this Special Agency under my charge…"

On November 22nd, 1963 President John F. Kennedy was touring downtown Dallas, Texas, in an open limousine. At 12:30 hours, a shooter opened fire. Two bullets from the rifle wounded Kennedy in the neck and head. When he arrived at the hospital he was dead.

Lee Harvey Oswald, a 24 year-old Dallas resident, was charged with murder. Two days later, Oswald, in turn, was murdered in the basement of the police station.

Kennedy's assassination is still the subject of controversy and speculation.

THE MASTERMIND

Aburto asserted he acted alone, that no one sent him to do what he did, there was no one behind him. But no one believed him. Behind Aburto's hand there had to be a brain, and people thought they knew who it belonged to.

José Francisco Ruiz Massieu was appalled by the murder, to the extent that he did not leave his house in three days. He invited Mario Melgar Adalid to breakfast at his home in Avenida Gutiérrez Zamora. When Melgar arrived, Ruiz Massieu was in the garden. The talk necessarily touched upon Colosio's death. In this regard, Ruiz Massieu called Claudia his daughter with Adriana Salinas, niece of Carlos Salinas de Gortari, and asked "Who are your friends saying is responsible for the death of Colosio?" Claudia answered with a question "My uncle Carlos?"

* * *

On November 28th, 1993, when the National Executive Committee of the PRI, publicly announced that Colosio was its presidential candidate, Manuel Camacho Solis, the losing candidate, reacted with complete disagreement. Breaking the party's discipline, he refused to accept the result and did not congratulate Colosio. His behavior showed that he did not think the fight was over and that he would continue trying to be the presidential candidate.

On January 1st 1994, an armed group in the state of Chiapas attacked the Mexican army, declaring war. That uprising polarized national and international attention and, of course, affected Colosio's campaign plans.

On January 10th, Colosio began his campaign in Huejutla, Hidalgo, with a brief and lackluster act. That same day, the President of the Republic named Manuel Camacho Solis, the loser in the search for the PRI nomination, as Commissioner for Peace in Chiapas.

From that moment on, all the media attention was focused on the negotiations with the Zapatistas in San Cristóbal de las Casas. Camacho's political stature grew as Colosio's campaign progressed hesitantly. In late February and early March, gossip was that Colosio would resign and Camacho would be appointed in his place. Salinas felt compelled to intervene to stop the rumors. In a meeting with PRI members he said: "In order to avoid confusion and to be clear, let me use the colloquial expression: Do not get tied up in knots! The PRI has the candidate that will take it to democratic victory. The Mexicans' vote will make Luis Donaldo Colosio succeed democratically."

On March 6th, a ceremony took place at the Monument to the Revolution to celebrate the 65th anniversary of the PRI. Colosio was the speaker, and this was his chance to strengthen his campaign. The critical tone of the speech and the fact that Colosio did not mention the President lead some to interpret that the speech was a break between the two.

* * *

Others adopted an opposite hypothesis, that: Colosio was Salinas' creature, he was his heir. The bullet that killed Colosio had destroyed Salinas' power. Salinas' enemies were behind the crime.

Others fixed their eyes upon Camacho.

Others on drug traffic.

Others... everyone had their favorite hypothesis. The only thing they agreed upon was that it had not been, and could not be a lone murderer.

* * *

Montes' resignation put an end to my role as consultant. The courts' summer holiday was starting as well. I decided to take a trip to Europe. On July 14th, 1994, at the airport, in the final waiting room, a TV screen projected President Salinas' image, reading a document: he reported that Montes, who considered he had accomplished a substantial part of the tasks he had been entrusted with, had resigned to his office as Assistant Attorney General. He thanked him and his team for the tasks performed. But he insisted: "The case is not closed nor the investigation is completed." He designated Olga Islas Magallanes de González Mariscal, Doctor of Law, with a solid career in the field of law enforcement, career teacher, holder of the Chair of Criminal Law at the National Autonomous University of Mexico and President of the Mexican Academy of Criminal Science, to continue the investigation. In addition, the President appointed a group of experts to advise Islas: Sergio García Ramírez, Jesús Zamora Pierce, Francisco Acuña Griego and Agustín Santamarina. It was obvious that the President wanted to strengthen the value of Islas' conclusions with the advice and the undoubted prestige of Ocuña Griego and Santamarina, but above all, with the figure of García Ramírez, who had been Attorney General, was a distinguished academic and an internationally renowned lawyer.

Islas was in a cruise in the Caribbean, at the time celebrating one of her granddaughters 15th birthday. Even there the presidential will reached her, forcing her to return to Mexico. On July 18th she accepted the position as Special Assistant Attorney.

In August, upon my return to Mexico, I joined the advisory group. Islas, together with her advisors, had set the goal of investigating a number of issues that could lead to evidence of the participation of others in the crime. In addition, it was necessary to continue with the ongoing processes, even when the person responsible thereof was still Marco Antonio Díaz de León.

On October 31st, 1994, Judge Alejandro Sosa Ortiz sentenced Aburto to forty-two years in prison for the charges of homicide with malice and premeditation, and possession of a firearm without a license. On December 22nd, 1994, in the appeal, the conviction was confirmed and the sentence was increased to forty-five years in prison.

On December 30th, 1994, just before the change of administration, Islas gave her final report. She considered that, out of the 31 investigation lines that she had proposed, she had solved 21, which had not provided any new elements that would allow to identify other responsible parties.

The lines that had been exhausted were:

2.- Statements of those who had had contact with Aburto during his arrest, transfer or examination.
4.- The report of all flights arriving or leaving Tijuana the day before, on the day, or the day after the fact.
5.- Investigation of the filming of the political meeting by the agents of the Federal Judicial Police.
6.- Investigation of the person who authorized the projection of the video to Aburto, prior to rendering his ministerial statement, and his motives.
7.- Investigation on the distribution of the video.
8.- Detailed investigation of Aburto's life in Tijuana.
9.- Investigation of the relationship that Aburto had with the people listed in the documents found in a trunk.
11.- Investigation of Aburto's relationship with Dr. Ernesto González Messina.
12.- Investigation on the co-defendants Tranquilino Sánchez, Vicente Mayoral and Rodolfo Mayoral.
13.- Psychological and social studies of the defendants, as well as of other people who were part of the organization and security or surveillance of the PRI meeting.
14.- New psychiatric study of Mario Aburto.
16.- Filing new evidence of the reconstruction of facts in the process.

18.- Verification of Aburto's identity.
19.- Location of the red-capped cameraman who appears in the video that was analyzed by the Spanish experts.
20.- Statement of Mr. Moisés Prats, who was present in the first hours when Aburto was examined.
21.- Analysis of the available data together with the co-director of the weekly newspaper *Zeta*.
22.- Conversation with those who could have any knowledge about the political gathering, the captures or the investigations in order to learn any reflection, fact or circumstance that could suggest or determine new investigation lines.
23.- Psychiatric and psychological analysis of a possible treatment for Aburto.
25.- Statement by Mario Luis Fuentes, who spoke with Colosio at the meeting.
28.- Statement of Mr. Colosio's campaign Public Relations Director.
29.- Analysis of the statements made by Miguel Eduardo Valle Espinosa.

On December 1st, 1994, Ernesto Zedillo Ponce de León took office as the new President of the Republic. He appointed Antonio Lozano Gracia as Attorney General. He offered the special attorney's office to Juan Velásquez, who had been advisor to Colosio's widow. Velázquez did not accept, but he told Lozano that the best investigator he knew was Pablo Chapa Bezanilla. Lozano got Zedillo to appoint Chapa as Special Attorney General for the Colosio, Juan Jesús Posadas Ocampo and José Francisco Ruiz Massieu cases. He took office on December 16th, 1994.

Aburto had already been convicted. Continuing with the investigation was only justified based on the search for other possible perpetrators: accomplices or the mastermind.

* * *

On February 22nd, 1996, on instructions from Chapa Bezanilla, Aburto was proposed to undergo a gas-therapy procedure. This technique consists on having the patient inhaling, through a mask, a mix of gases with 70% oxygen and 30% carbon dioxide, which causes him a shallow sleep in order to evoke memories not consciously accepted. Aburto accepted, and the process began under the control of two psychiatrists, however, once the session had started, he sat up and removed the mask. They proposed and he accepted a second session, which took place on February 23rd. This time, one of the psychiatrists volunteered to carry out the procedure, in order to instill confidence in him. Then, Aburto relaxed and leaned back on a couch and the mask was placed on him for ten minutes. Finally, when he was under a light sleep state, psychiatrists examined him. Aburto insisted that he acted alone, that nobody paid him to kill Colosio.

This test has no legal value, but by accepting to submit to it, Aburto showed that he was not afraid of revealing a truth that he could have been hiding.

* * *

A couple of months into the job, Chapa Bezanilla provided bombshell news: There was a second shooter!

* * *

Shortly after 17:00 hours on March 23rd, 1994, Raúl Loza Parra, deputy delegate of the Federal Judicial Police, who was in the Attorney General's Office, received on his cell phone a call from Alfredo Aarón Juárez Jiménez, who had been delegate of the Attorney General's Office in the state of Baja California. Juárez Jiménez, who was in Lomas Taurinas, informed him that Colosio had suffered an attack and that, precisely where Juárez Jiménez was standing, there was a bullet in a pool of blood, and he asked him to go to Lomas Taurinas to retrieve the bullet. Loza Parra resolved to go to Lomas Taurinas, but at that time the vehicles that were bringing Aburto and Tranquilino arrived, with open siren, at the Attorney General's Office. Loza Parra had to meet the detainees and he was not able to leave immediately for Lomas Taurinas.

Juárez Jiménez, by his own knowledge, even without being an expert, thought that the bullet was caliber thirty-eight. As many people passed and trod on the blood, he organized a barrier to protect the pool of blood, so nobody would touch the bullet while the police or the Prosecution arrived. Then, the people who were making up the barrier put up a small stone fence to mark off the area.

Later, on instructions from Fernando de la Sota Rodalléguez, coordinator of the Order, Fences and Cheerleading group, Rigoberto Flores González, a municipal police officer from the city of Tijuana and Alejandro García Hinojosa, member of the candidate's personnel escort, moved to Lomas Taurinas. Flores González got a plastic spatula from the people and lifted the bullet with the attached blood and dirt and put it into a polyethylene bag. Then they went to the Attorney General's Office, where they delivered it to Fernando de la Sota Rodalléguez.

Between 01:00 and 02:00 hours on March 24th, 1994 the Director General of Expert Services, Miguel Oscar Aguilar Ruiz and the expert in ballistics José Luis Pérez Zamora arrived at the Attorney General's office. On instructions from the latter, the bullet was washed. In order to determine if the bullet had been fired by Aburto's gun, it was necessary to have a micro comparison report, but the necessary equipment was not available in Tijuana. Aguilar Ruiz then ordered Zamora Pérez to travel to Mexico City to get the report.

The result of the expert studies was that the bullet retrieved from the crime scene had been in fact shot by
Aburto's revolver and, most probably, was the one that hurt the candidate in the abdomen, which explains why it did not lose its aerodynamic profile, since it did not hit any hard tissues.

If the bullet that injured Colosio in the abdomen was shot by Aburto's revolver that means that there was not, there couldn't be, a second shooter. That bullet was an insurmountable obstacle to support the thesis that there was a second shooter. But not for Chapa Bezanilla. He said that he had asked his assistants to shoot a gun (not Aburto's) on land (not at Lomas Taurinas) against a pigskin. The bullet, after passing through the skin, had penetrated into the ground and suffered various deformations. Based on that experience, Chapa Bezanilla stated that the bullet found in Lomas Taurinas had been *sown*. He could never prove this statement.

The bullet that injured Colosio in the abdomen left an entry orifice and an exit orifice in his body. It also left an entry orifice in the jacket he was wearing, but not an exit orifice. Prosecutor González, in his final report, states: "The forensic analysis of the jacket that the candidate wore on the day of the meeting indicated that the average angle of incidence of the injury due to the shot in the abdomen corresponds to the entry orifice on the left side of the garment and the tear observed in the inner right part, where, most probably, the bullet remained lodged, since should it had followed the path, there would be an exit orifice, which does not exist, on the right outside part of the jacket. In order to confirm or refute the hypothesis, the mechanics of helping candidate Colosio after he was injured were simulated, by placing a .38" special bullet in the internal tear of the jacket. It should be noted that the inner linings of this garment are open as if they were inverted pockets. The body of the person who served as monitor was placed in a ventral decubitus position and he rose representing the way in which Mr. Colosio was lifted. The exercise was performed ten times, and nine out of the ten the bullet fell to the floor, and four times it was located in what pretended to be the blood pool, where various witnesses relate they had seen it. Hence, the high probability that the bullet recovered from the scene had been initially housed in the right inner side of the jacket, to then fall to the place where it was found. In this regard, and with the support of a tailor, a jacket with the same characteristics as the garment worn by Luis Donaldo Colosio Murrieta was reproduced (size, type of fabric, color, cut) to support in the performance of the different recreation exercises. However, and in order to have more reliable results, the final exercises were carried out using the jacket that the candidate had been wearing at the time of the crime."

* * *

Colosio was shot twice: the first time in the skull, with a right-to-left path and the second time in the abdomen, left-to-right. How could Aburto be the author of both shots? The experts from the Montes prosecution office, studying the victim-offender position, stated that: a) at the time of the first shot, Aburto was on the right side of the candidate, slightly behind him, b) when receiving the impact of the first shot, the body of the candidate turned about 90° to the left, while the murderer, simultaneously, made a slight shift to the north, c) this change in the position of the victim and the victimizer explains why the second shot penetrated the abdomen from the left.

Chapa rejected the theory of the 90° turn, which imposed the conclusion that there had been two shooters: one from the right and another from the left. On February 24th, 1995, the Attorney General's Office exercised criminal action against Othón Cortés Vázquez accusing him of being the second shooter. The accusation was based on the testimony of three people: María Belem Mackliz Romero, Jorge Romero Romero and Jorge Amaral Muñoz, who identified him as the person who was on the candidate's left side with a firearm. The latter even said he saw him shoot.

* * *

Othón Cortés was a humble man, without a trade, who made his living by being the *gofer* for politicians. He was the one carrying bags, the one who gets the soft drinks, drives the car, whatever is needed. He told journalist Guillermo Osorno that he went to Lomas Taurinas "to be seen, in order to be offered a job." Osorno tells that, when Colosio came down from the platform, Othón Cortés walked behind him. After the attack he ran behind the people who were carrying Colosio's body and boarded a car that took him to the General Hospital. He arrived there almost at the same time as the ambulance and helped to bring the stretcher out and to move Colosio up to the door of the building. Without being asked, he closed the hospital door and stayed there as guard. He faced the crowd that wanted to go in, until the municipal police arrived... Cortés learned of Colosio's death in the hospital. A little later, a person from the PRI National Executive Committee approached him and told him they needed him to drive the front car of the procession taking Colosio's body to the airport. They gave him the vehicle keys. Cortés took the car around the block, cleaned it, checked the oil, got in and fell asleep. Around one o'clock in the morning someone knocked on the window. "Let's go" he was told. A group of people, García Reyes among them, got into the car. Someone took a picture, which would later serve as evidence that the general and Cortés knew each other. He drove up to the airport and said goodbye to the group that took the flight back to Mexico City. From day one, he thought that Aburto was the only one responsible of the murder. "For a conspiracy, you need smart people," he said, "not a poor gay as the Mayorals, or me." One year and a half later he was driving his children to school together with his wife when a car stopped them. Some men got out and asked him "Othón Cortés?" He was arrested and taken to a security house where he was blindfolded and handcuffed. After having him tied for hours, they beat him into a car and took him to Mexicali, where a plane from the PGR was waiting. They arrived in Mexico City and took him to the prosecutor's office in Insurgentes. He was told there that they knew about the second shot, that they would help to lessen the sentence, but that he had to confess that Manlio Fabio Beltrones, García Reyes and Del Pozo were involved. Cortés refused to sign the confession. He received a blow that broke his eardrum."

* * *

Jorge Romero Romero, Jorge Amaral Muñoz and María Belem Mackliz Romero had already declared several times before the Attorney General's Office, and they had never mentioned Othon Cortés. Until Chapa Bezanilla arrived.

Mackliz, in her first statement, on April 28th, 1994, stated that "...she did not see who fired the shots..." On February 23rd, 1995 Chapa Bezanilla summoned her to extend her statement, when she arrived "...I was introduced to Mr. Chapa Bezanilla, and he told me that I was going to make an extension to my statement. Chapa Bezanilla and the agent were talking very suspiciously, away from me and whispering, then Mr. Chapa said "come here, Ms. Mackliz" and the agent led me to the upper part of the offices, inside a regular size office, the agent started drafting what would be my alleged statement, he never questioned me, once he finished he gave me the document that was drafted to sign. When I read this document, I realized that the text said that I fully identified Othón Cortés Vázquez, as well as the fact that it stated that the fire gun was pointed at Mr. Colosio's left side, I was dissatisfied and told him I would not sign. Then the agent went down and Mr. Chapa Bezanilla came upstairs and told me to sign, that there was no problem with those details... "

On April 18th, 1994, Jorge Romero Romero, stated that "...he couldn't see Mr. Colosio's perpetrator..." Chapa Bezanilla's agents showed him some videos and pictures of what had happened at Lomas Taurinas. They explained to him what he had actually seen. Under the prosecutors' pressure, Romero starts to believe that he saw what they say he saw and, on February 23rd, 1995, when he is shown a photocopy of an ID badge belonging to Othón Cortés, he says "he has the same physiognomy as the person that has been identified as placing the gun to the candidate's left side."

Jorge Amaral Muñoz, on August 20th, 1994, declared that the day of the incident he was at Lomas Taurinas and after the meeting, he heard two shots, but "...he did not see Mario Aburto shooting or someone shooting Mr. Colosio..." But, called by Chapa Bezanilla, on February 9th, 1995, he could remember that a man standing alongside "on the candidate's left side … shoots him on the left side", since he can picture the gun barrel and the left side of the person making the shot; that he had visibility "because when the first shot happens the people open up and run, others crouch … ", and finally "... having nine color photographs before him, labeled with numbers from 1 to 9, in the first one, enlarged, he notes that he fully identifies the subject as the one he saw making the shot (Othón Cortés) ... that he identifies that guy without any doubt as the same one he saw shooting Colosio's body on the left side ... "

On August 7th, 1996 Othón Cortés was acquitted and released. The falseness of the witnesses the prosecution rested on was evident. Furthermore, during the process, a film showing what had happened in Lomas Taurinas was screened. It could be seen that Othón Cortés' right hand rests on General Domiro Garcia Reyes' left shoulder at the time of the first shot, so it was impossible, that he could take out a gun and shoot with that hand almost simultaneously.

* * *

The Attorney General's Office exercised penal action against

Romero, Amaral and Mackliz, for the crime of false statements in court. The Fifth District Judge in the State of Baja California, located in Tijuana, issued an arrest warrant against Romero and Amaral, and refused to issue one against Mackliz, considering she had not incurred in willful misconduct. Romero was arrested, indicted and sentenced to prison, Amaral fled to the United States where he was arrested and subject to deportation proceedings.

Chapa Bezanilla, discredited, was deprived of the Special Prosecutor position on August 30th, 1996. He was the only one of the four special prosecutors who, at the end of his term, did not leave a written report of his work.

On August 31st, 1996, President Zedillo appointed the fourth and last man to hold the position: Luis Raúl González Pérez, who had experience in investigation works as Inspector General of the National Human Rights Commission.

* * *

When González took office, there were no ongoing criminal procedures. In the prosecution offices, now located on Río Rhin street, the atmosphere was more like an academic cloister than a police station. And indeed, González got himself the highest level scientists to guide his investigations. For example, and only in order to determine the mechanics and time of Colosio's fall, he requested the support and collaboration of the Physics and Astronomy Institute, the School of Medicine and the Film Library of UNAM, the National Neurology and Neurosurgery Institute of the Ministry of Health, prominently, the National Nuclear Research Institute, the Attorney General of the Federal District, the Ministry of National Defense, the Federal Bureau of Investigation (FBI) and the Arms Factory Forjas Taurus, from Brazil . The conclusion: Colosio's body turned 90 degrees.

González also focused on the old issue of *the two Aburtos*, and found an imaginative and original way to solve it: an expert opinion on speech therapy and another one related to the identification of bloodstains. The first one was a comparative study of the audios recorded during Aburto's examination, on March 23rd, 1994, in Tijuana; the corresponding video of the scenes of his ministerial statement, on March 23rd, the audio cassette of the police interrogation during his transfer from the prefecture of the PGR to Tijuana's airport on March 24th, and the video of the reconstruction of facts that took place at the penitentiary of Almoloya on September 16th, 1994. The examination of these audio elements led to the conclusion by expert, Dr. Severino Tarasco Camino, that the voices presented the same basic elements: timbre, resonance, pitch and melody. That is, they were issued by the same person.

The expert's opinion on bloodstains identification consisted on examining those that stained the black jacket that Aburto was wearing on March 23rd, which resulted from the head injuries that the crowd inflicted on him, and to compare them with Aburto's blood, which, according to his medical records in Almoloya is "O" Rh positive. The expert examination showed the already known result: Aburto is Aburto, is Aburto, is Aburto...

* * *

González' main job was studying what he called "*The political environment* generated for Luis Donaldo Colosio, first by the conflict in Chiapas and immediately after by the appointment of Mr. Manuel Camacho Solís as Honorary Commissioner for Peace in that state, as well as the minor coverage of his campaign in the national press, leading to the interpretation that there had been a break between the candidate and the President of the Republic, and that the latter was seeking to replace him and would have orchestrated a press campaign against him to weaken him. The next step, according to the hypothesis, was elimination, with the complacency of those in charge of protecting him, for not agreeing to give up the candidacy. This is, in short, the speculative picture on which the political motive or "State crime" theory of the murder of Luis Donaldo Colosio is based."

Montes and Islas had looked for the mastermind starting with Aburto and his surroundings, trying to find the traces that would allow them to detect his presence. González acted conversely. He went up directly to those, who, if rumors were true, could have some responsibility.

"In an Orthodox investigation", he said "inquiries are based on concomitant circles around the perpetrator and we have done so with extreme diligence. But we are also aware that given the social and political impact of the crime, there have been multiple signs that could put in a relative perspective any conclusion, if they are not observed, therefore we have also investigated and clarified them. This has meant that, unlike other cases in the world, we have been open to all kinds of data and information, even those which at first might seem unlikely and that attention was given to doubts and opinions expressed in books or newspaper publications, in order not to risk missing any clues that could lead to the truth."

This method led González to seek the truth by questioning those who had participated in the investigation before, including: Diego Valadés Ríos, Miguel Montes García, Olga Islas Magallanes, José Pablo Chapa Bezanilla, Rafael Moreno González, Carlos Tornero Díaz, Jesús Zamora Pierce and Mario Croswell.

Points of view were also exchanged and interviews were held with:

Daniel Acosta Cázares, Jorge Alcocer, Jazmín Alessandrini, Alberto Anaya, Hugo Andrés Araujo, Leonel Argüelles Méndez, Federico Arreola Castillo, Pedro Aspe Armella, Walter Asthie, Agustín Basave Benítez, Manlio Fabio Beltrones Rivera, Humberto Benítez Treviño, Marco Antonio Bernal Gutiérrez, María Bernal Romero, Jesús Blancornelas, Gilberto Borja Navarrete, Juan Burgos Pinto, Josie Burgos, Ricardo Canavati Tafich, Fernando Cantú, Cuauhtémoc Cárdenas Solórzano, José Ramón Carreño Carlón, Marcos Castillejos, Luis Colosio Fernández, Luis Romeo Colosio Miranda, Dalia Conde, David Dafni, Melchor de los Santos Ordóñez, Enrique Del Val Blanco, Luis Raúl Domínguez, Alfonso Durazo Montaño, Juan Francisco Ealy Ortiz, Marcelo Ebrard, Edgar Elías Azar, Guillermo Espinoza Velazco, Óscar Espinosa Villarreal, Ricardo Franco Guzmán, Mario Ignacio Frías Valenzuela, Mario Luis Fuentes Alcalá, Francisco Galindo Ochoa, Heriberto Galindo Quiñones, Emilio Gamboa Patrón, Fernando Gamboa Rosas,

Domiro García Reyes and Javier García Ávila.

As well as Leonel Godoy Rangel, Fernando Gómez Mont, Claudio X. González, Germán González Castillo, Patrocinio González Garrido, René González de la Vega, Roberto González Barrera, Miguel Ángel Granados Chapa, Alejandro Gurza, Fernando Gutiérrez Barrios, Humberto Hernández Haddad, Silvia Hernández, Guillermo Hopkins Gámez, Enrique Jackson Ramírez, Manuel Jiménez Guzmán, William Karam, Nikita Kyriakis, Nora la Calle, Roberta Lajous, Joaquín Legarreta, Nereyda López, María Angélica Luna Parra, Jorge R. Mancillas, Enrique Márquez, Luis Martínez Fernández del Campo, Jaime Martínez Veloz, Andrés Massieu Berlanga, Héctor Mayer Soto, Aquiles Medellín, Mario Melgar Adalid, Antonio Meza Estrada, Jorge Montaño Martínez, Jorge Moreno Collado, Rafael Oceguera Ramos, Benito Ohara Inukai and Carlos Amado Olmos Tomasini.

Also, Santiago Oñate Laborde, Roberto Ortega Lomelí, Antonio Ortíz Mena, Fernando Ortíz Arana, Armando Pacheco González, José de Jesús Padilla Padilla, Samuel Palma César, Beatriz Paredes Rangel, José Luis Pérez Canchola, Héctor Pérez Vargas, Stanley A. Pimentel, Ramiro Pineda Murguía, Frank S. Quijada, Alfonso Ramos, Salvador Rangel Medina, Enrique Régules Uriegas, Rafael Reséndiz Contreras, Hilda Elisa Riojas Reyes, Rodrigo Riojas Reyes, Teresa Ríos Rico, Fernanda Riveroll, Eduardo Robledo Rincón, Salvador Rocha Díaz, Amador Rodríguez Lozano, Ernesto Ruffo Appel, Armando Ruíz Massieu, Roberto Salcedo Aquino, Cuauhtémoc Sánchez Ocio, César Augusto Santiago, Jaime Serra Puche, Ivar Sisniega Campbell, José Luis Soberanes Reyes, Israel Soberanis Nogueda, Javier Treviño Cantú, José Asunción Ureña Velázquez, Misael Uribe Esquivel, Eduardo Valle Espinosa, Glenn W. Mactaggart, Enrique Wolper Barraza y Raúl Zorrilla Cossio.

Finally, in an unprecedented act in the history of Mexico, statements were requested and obtained from President Ernesto Zedillo Ponce de León, who had been General Coordinator of Colosio's campaign, and two ex-presidents Carlos Salinas de Gortari and Luis Echeverría Álvarez.

"In this way," says González "and after more than six years of investigations, the preliminary investigation that was prepared on the homicide of Luis Donaldo Colosio Murrieta comprises 174 volumes, containing 68,293 pages plus 293 annexes. The prosecutor has heard the statements of 1,460 people and 533 have expanded their statements, making a total of 1,993 statements. Around 551 reports have been requested from various authorities, the Federal Judicial Police has conducted 982 investigations and 326 expert opinions have been rendered."

This investigation is the deepest that has been made on an assassination, both regarding its duration and cost, as for the relevance of the scientific support, as well as the number of people who contributed to the investigation or testified as witnesses.

But the result has left us parked in the solitary murderer.

In his final report, submitted late in 2000, González says:

"All avenues of investigation that we have followed have been addressed in depth and, to date, none has proved a serious element linking to other perpetrators. The investigation, in itself, is a true reflection that we have always favored the search for other possible participants and, while some suspicions were valid as a starting point, one cannot hope to build on them without further evidence than speculation, the flimsy building that gives support to social expectation, at the risk of seeing it miserably collapsing again.

The Prosecution prosecutes crimes and suspects and from the procedures so far there have not been any elements to support charges against anyone, as alleged accomplice or instigator of Mario Aburto to execute the crime, or that someone besides him agreed or prepared its realization. Had it been the case, we would have proceeded immediately to consign him before the courts."

Back in July 1994, Montes, in his final report, had said:

"As a result of its work, the Special Deputy Attorney was able to fully prove, beyond reasonable doubt, that the material and intellectual author of the murder is Mario Aburto Martínez, who acted alone, long premeditated his crime and attributed his action to political motivation... Logically, there is always the possibility that new evidence arises. I think there is a very slim possibility that such new evidence, should it exist, would require changing the conclusions reached today by the Special Deputy Attorney under my charge..."

"Yes, if only for the interest of all, I have to do it or die," he thought. "Yes, I will approach... and then suddenly, with pistol or dagger? That does not matter! "It is not me, it is the hand of fate that punishes you," I will say, he thought, imagining what he would say when he killed Napoleon. "Well, take me and kill me," he continued, speaking to himself and bowing his head with a sad but firm expression."

War and Peace.

Tolstoy.

APPENDIX

Conspirator or lone assassin?

The conquest of power or its exercise affects interests. The powerful lives surrounded by those who, for economic, social, ideological, political or religious reasons, are his enemies.

If an assassination occurs, immediately forefingers pointing to the possible father of the conspiracy will rise. The idea that behind the crime there is a mastermind, is indestructible, since, logically, it is impossible to prove that the murder is NOT the result of a conspiracy.

Could Aburto be the puppet of an evil brain that decided the destruction of Colosio? Yes, this hypothesis fits into the vast world of the *possible*. But in order to support this hypothesis, we must accept that the mastermind was, both very clever and very clumsy.

Very clever, because he achieved his purpose: the death of Colosio. And besides, he committed the perfect crime, he was able to hide himself, so that the investigation of Montes, Islas and González, under various Mexican Presidents, for six years, with all the resources of criminology, failed to find him. His talent also led him to select the perfect assassin, who repeated over and over again: "I acted alone, behind me there is no one," who has spent twenty years of his life in prison and who is preparing to spend twenty-five years more there.

That dark spirit is also someone with luck, none of the links in the chain that binds him to the perpetrator has broken. No one has confessed his involvement, pressed by questions from the prosecution. No one made a mistake that would allow prosecutors to confront him with the truth. No one, near death, decided to clear his chest of accumulated guilt.

But the genius, at the same time, committed unpardonable blunders. Being able to hire professional murderers, he chose citizen zero. He gave him an old revolver, with capacity for six cartridges, loaded with only four. That shoddy hit man left evidence everywhere of what he would do. The day of the crime, he appeared on time to do his job, he checked in and, after finishing his shift, he asked where was the place that would be the stage where he had an appointment with destiny. He allowed to be arrested at the scene of the crime. No one killed him. He confessed his crime and today, twenty years later, is still alive.

Aburto is the archetypal assassin. Accepting the hypothesis of the lone murderer presents yet another problem: our mind assumes the cause should be as important as the effect. Colosio could only be destroyed by someone as important or more important than him. If we admit that citizen zero was able to arrive, amidst numerous armed guards, taking the life of the candidate for President of the Republic and change the history of Mexico, then we must recognize that any trivial cause, in a second, can annihilate us, destroy everything we are. This is unacceptable ... but it's true..

ABOUT THE AUTHOR

Jesús Zamora Pierce has been a lawyer for more than 52 years, practicing criminal law in México. He was president of the Barra Mexicana de Abogados (lawyer association in Mexico), President of the Academia Mexicana de Ciencias Penales (most prestigious legal science organization in Mexico), winner of the Premio Nacional de Jurisprudencia (national law award), has published tens of criminal law books in Mexico, and many of his books are mandatory texts in colleges and higher level education institutions in Mexico.

Made in the USA
Columbia, SC
11 January 2025